BIBLE PRAYING

Also edited by Michael Perry

The Daily Bible
Church Family Worship
Carols for Today
Carol Praise
Prayers for the People
The Dramatised Bible
Psalms for Today
The Wedding Book
Songs from the Psalms
Dramatised Bible Readings for Festivals

BIBLE PRAYING

Michael Perry

Fount
An Imprint of HarperCollins*Publishers*

First published in Great Britain
in 1992 by Fount Paperbacks

Fount Paperbacks is an imprint of
HarperCollinsReligious
Part of HarperCollins*Publishers*
77–85 Fulham Palace Road, London W6 8JB

Printed and bound in Great Britain by
HarperCollinsManufacturing Glasgow

A catalogue record for this book
is available from the British Library

To Beatrice, my wife,
who has supported me
in the writing of many books
but never yet
had one dedicated to her,
with my love.

CONTENTS

PREFACE

PURPOSE OF THE PRAYERS

Many of the best prayers in our heritage of English liturgy derive from the Old and New Testaments. Thomas Cranmer and his peers were masters of the technique of creatively using the scriptures to express what worshippers needed to say. Indeed, many Bible texts and passages became well-known simply because they were often repeated in the form of prayers. The most obvious demonstration of this is within the 1662 *Book of Common Prayer* service of Holy Communion.

All denominations since the Reformation have benefited from this unremembered development – the sourcing of prayers in scripture texts; for the 'BCP' prayers have become a model for much of our praying ecumenically. Now, when churches are once again experimenting with new liturgies, we can look again to the Bible's riches to formulate our prayers. *Bible Praying* suggests an approach, and offers over 500 examples of what is possible.

The Church of England's Liturgical Commission in its Synodical publication 'Patterns for Worship' reaffirmed its predecessor's *ASB 1980* commitment to 'flexibility' in worship forms. 'The minister may . . . in these or other words' is a permissive rubric we shall encounter increasingly. The biblical prayers of our *Church Family Worship* (Hodder & Stoughton) have been seized upon for wide use in the purely adult, as well as the family, context – so much so that we have been led to develop further material for congregations in the two editions of *Prayers for the People*, (People's Edition and Leaders' Edition, HarperCollins). Here in *Bible Praying* many more prayers specifically based on Bible text are available for use.

I have deliberately avoided using any one translation in preparing these prayers, though, inevitably there will be unintended echoes of contemporary versions. It is important that we avoid trespassing on copyrights, though usually copyright owners are generous in the permissions they give, as long as this does not mean a wholesale lifting of text.

It is hoped that clergy and ministers will feel free not only to reproduce and use the material in *Bible Praying*, but also to try their hand at creating their own Bible prayers in the categories suggested by the chapter headings.

In the developing world, also, there is a pressing need for churches to develop *indigenous* forms of worship. Ministers and clergy usually have access to Bibles in their own language, and do not need great skill to create prayers from Bible text – just some examples of how it can be done, the encouragement to try, and the permission to use the results in public worship. How much better that they do this than translate western English prayers written for a different culture and in a remote situation!

ARRANGEMENT OF THE PRAYERS

Each separate chapter of *Bible Praying* draws together prayers with the same function in worship; for instance, confessions are arranged together in one chapter, absolutions in another. The chapters follow each other in a sequence that corresponds to the customary – often necessary – order of worship: the chapter of absolutions follows the chapter of confessions.

Within each chapter, individual prayers are arranged according to the Bible books from which they are derived. For instance, a thanksgiving based on a passage from *Isaiah* will follow thanksgivings derived from the *Psalms*.

This logical arrangement gives speedy access to the prayer that is wanted without the need to refer to an index. Two indexes are available – the first is a Season and Subject index and the second a Bible Reference index.

The Season and Subject index affords users of *Bible Praying* the opportunity to match prayers to themes and occasions; the Bible Reference index relates prayers to passages under consideration.

DESCRIPTION OF THE PRAYERS

Here follow brief descriptions of the material contained in each of the chapters, and some indication of its potential use:

Greeting *(Numbers 1–32)* Many of the New Testament epistles begin with a greeting; each writer who intended that his letter should be read out to a congregation, salutes in the name of the Lord the people to whom he is about to address his message. Such greetings are frequently suitable for contemporary worship, either at the beginning of a service or at The Peace in Holy Communion. As with each of the prayers in *Bible Praying*, indications are given as to appropriate use – seasonal and topical.

Approach *(Numbers 33–61)* These prayers are offered as an introduction for worshippers – as an 'Approach to God' or, more generally, as 'Approach to Worship'. They state what we are about as we come together for prayer, praise, adoration, thanksgiving, intercession, and communion with all the saints and with our Lord.

Commandment *(Numbers 62–68)* Included here are one or two responsive prayers and declarations intended purely for congregational use. There are further examples in subsequent sections, others in our *Church Family Worship* (Hodder & Stoughton) and many more in both minister's and leaders' editions of *Prayers for the People* (HarperCollins).

Confession *(Numbers 69–100)* Words of confession, in public worship most appropriately said by everyone present, are assembled from the scripture text to meet the needs of various situations. Some of them are fairly specific in their reference and should not casually be put into the mouths of worshippers, but when the circumstances are right and with careful application. As with most of the prayers in *Bible Praying*, private devotional use is also appropriate.

Absolution *(Numbers 101–162)* The declaration of forgiveness – which comes from God with the authority of Christ – is spoken by the minister and received by the Christian as part of that regeneration and renewal which is the beginning of spiritual life and its constant accompaniment. Forms of absolution are drawn from various passages, and suited to many contexts in the worshippers' experience. The option is given – either by an italicized *you* or by an alternative version of the prayer – for the language of the first person to be used: 'Lord forgive *me* . . .', etc.

Exhortation *(Numbers 163–194)* The only English exhortations which are widely known, but now in decline, are the traditional ones, of which the phrases, 'Dearly belov-ed bretheren . . .', and 'Let us in heart and mind go even unto Bethlehem' are evocative. Here is a rich fund of alternatives.

Introduction/Conclusion (Readings) *(Numbers 195–200)* This section adds a little biblical variety to what is normally said in worship at the announcement or conclusion of a Reading.

Creed *(Numbers 201–232)* From the Latin 'Credo' ('I believe'). In use, a creed becomes more a *declaration of faith* than a statement of doctrine as intended in the historical context of ecclesiastical controversy. In other words, Christians now do not want to emphasize their orthodoxy but to affirm the truths of their faith and, even more importantly, to acclaim the God in whom they put their trust. Early Christian creeds were both teaching statements and triumphant declarations.

The attempt to recite in worship the whole gamut of our

Religion is as futile as it is dreary. It is refreshing to be able to use once again some of the simple forms of creed in the New Testament, and to do so with proper regard to the subject of the service or the season of the year. See, for example the *1 Corinthians 15* creed at number 211 – entirely appropriate for Easter; the *John 1* creed at number 204 – for Christmas; or the Unity creed at 217. The early creeds emerged from the freshness of conviction that God was incarnate in Christ, sharing our lot and redeeming our humanity, that he had died and risen for our salvation, that the Spirit had come as the seal of our redemption until the Saviour's return to take his people to glory. These assurances were repeated until they were 'rounded' in form and, through the apostles and the New Testament, became part and parcel of our Christian inheritance.

Somewhat adventurously in this chapter, three Old Testament texts are worked into credal form in the light of the Christian revelation, much as apostles, fathers and hymn writers have done throughout the Christian centuries.

Dedication/Commendation/Declaration *(Numbers 233–239)* This section groups together elements that do not need a section on their own. They envisage a situation where individuals are being dedicated or commissioned, and include 'catachetical' responses about Holy Communion and Baptism.

For others *(Numbers 240–255)* Obviously, the scope for deriving intercessions from the Bible text is strictly limited because the circumstances in which the need for such prayers arises is contemporary and so often specific. Nevertheless, some subjects never change; and in this section are to be found prayers about terrorism, the weak, the anxious, children and parenting, justice, the elderly, seafarers, mission, the dying, preachers, healers, and marriage.

For ourselves *(Numbers 256–330)* The Psalms are a fruitful source of meditation and prayer arising from individual and corporate spirituality. Prayers from the Psalms dominate this section. But there are also some gems from the Prophets and from the New Testament.

Thanksgiving *(Numbers 331–367)* There are thanksgivings here for special occasions: church anniversary or dedication, harvest, seasons of the Christian year, new year, missionary events, Holy Communion; and allied to special subjects such as creation, giving, redemption, forgiveness, answers to prayer, witness, renewal, and God's love and mercy.

Acclamation *(Numbers 368–376)* We acclaim God as sovereign, and praise him for what he has done. Here are nine additional texts devised for this purpose.

Doxology/Ascription *(Numbers 377–401)* From the Latin 'doxa' (glory). Doxology is a description of prayers which set forth the glory of God, and which use the word 'Glory' somewhere in the text. The *Ascriptions* also proclaim God's attributes and give him praise for them, but do not have the distinctive 'glory' of the doxologies. They are usefully separated because in public worship one Ascription and one Doxology could be used together, while two of either would be excessive.

Blessing *(Numbers 402–527)* Something more than a 'Benediction' and not necessarily 'pronouncing all things to be well', these blessings are based on exhortatory and encouraging scriptures, and given the classical form. They are usefully linked by the minister to passages which have been under consideration in service or sermon; and it is helpful to say where the blessing comes from when announcing it: 'We sit/*stand*/*kneel* for the Blessing, which comes from 1 Peter 5.'

Dismissal *(Numbers 528–534)* Contemporary English liturgies content themselves with simple dismissals, and no variety: 'Go in peace to love and serve the Lord', etc. The last items in the book offer additional suggestions for the minister. In Anglican churches it is the Deacon who properly says the Dismissal.

REPRODUCTION OF THE PRAYERS

Local copying and printing

The restriction on copying and typographic reproduction does not apply to the local use of individual items from this book. Author and publisher are happy for prayers to be reproduced for use in church services or other worship contexts, provided that the Bible reference is given at the head or foot of the prayer, and that reference is made somewhere in the document to *Bible Praying* as the source from which the prayer has been drawn.

Publication in other books

The prayers in *Bible Praying* are © *copyright 1992 Michael Perry,* and may be reproduced individually by permission in North America of **Hope Publishing Company, Carol Stream, Illinois 60188 (800–323–1049);** and in the rest of the world by permission of **Jubilate Hymns, 61 Chessel Avenue, Southampton SO2 4DY (0703 630038).**

It is hoped that *Bible Praying* will be equally accessible to the individual and to the congregation; to the individual as a resource for private devotion, to the congregation as an enhancement of worship. The traditional chapter titles are there to distinguish the uses of the prayers, not to mark them as peculiarly 'Anglican'. The contents of the book are commended ecumenically – to all denominations – for the glorious inheritance of the Old and New Testament scriptures we share alike.

Michael Perry
Tonbridge, All Saints 1991

GREETING

1 GREETING
Harvest, general
from Ruth 2

The Lord be with you:
the Lord bless you! Amen.

2 GREETING
Evening, ministry
from Psalm 134

All of you who serve the Lord;
who come in the evening of the day
to worship in his house,
who lift up your hands in his holy place
and praise the Lord:
may the Lord, the maker of heaven and earth,
bless you! **Amen.**

3 GREETING
Civic, general
from Romans 1

Grace and peace to you
from God our Father
and from the Lord Jesus Christ. **Amen.**

4 GREETING
Invitation to service, unity
from Romans 15

Welcome one another
as Christ has welcomed you:
to God be the glory. Amen.

5 GREETING
Civic, general
from Romans 15

The God of peace be with you all. **Amen.**

6 GREETING
Visiting
from 1 Corinthians 1

Visitor:
Greetings to the church of God in_____*,
called to be God's holy people
in Christ Jesus.

Host:
Greetings to all who know and love
the Lord Jesus Christ,
your Lord and ours.

Both:
God our Father
and the Lord Jesus Christ,
give you grace and peace. **Amen.**

7 GREETING
General
from 1 Corinthians 1 (variant)

Grace and peace to you
from God our Father
and Jesus Christ our Saviour. **Amen.**

(* Here the local name is supplied)

8 GREETING
Reconciliation
from 2 Corinthians 13

The God of love and peace be with you. **Amen.**

9 GREETING
General
from Galatians 1

Grace and peace to you
from God our Father
and the Lord Jesus Christ. **Amen.**

10 GREETING
Passiontide
from Galatians 1

Grace and peace be with you
from God our Father,
and the Lord Jesus Christ,
who gave himself for our sins
according to the will of God:
to whom be glory for ever and ever. **Amen.**

11 GREETING
Penitence, Lent, unity
from Galatians 6

Peace and mercy to the people of God. **Amen.**

12 GREETING
Mission, absence
from Ephesians 2

Peace to those who are near,
and peace to those who are far away. **Amen.**

13 GREETING
All Saints, Holy Communion, service
from Ephesians 6

Grace to all who love our Lord Jesus Christ
  with an undying love. **Amen.**

14 GREETING
Conference, ministry, general
from Ephesians 6

Peace to you,
brothers and sisters,
and love with faith;
from God the Father
and the Lord Jesus Christ. **Amen.**

15 GREETING
General, renewal
from Philippians 4 and Philemon

The grace of the Lord Jesus Christ
be with your spirit. **Amen.**

16 GREETING
General, visiting
from 1 Thessalonians 1

Grace and peace to you
from God our Father
and the Lord Jesus Christ. **Amen.**

17 GREETING
General
from 2 Timothy 1

Grace, mercy and peace,
from God the Father
and Christ Jesus our Lord. **Amen.**

18 GREETING
General
from 2 Timothy 4

The Lord be with your spirit:
grace and peace be with you. Amen.

19 GREETING
Civic, general
from Titus 1

Grace and peace
from God the Father
and Christ Jesus our saviour. **Amen.**

20 GREETING
General
from Titus 1 (variant)

May God the Father
and Christ Jesus our saviour
give you grace and peace. **Amen.**

21 GREETING
Visiting, unity
from Titus 3

Greetings, friends in the faith;
God's grace be with you all! **Amen.**

22 GREETING
General
from Philemon 1

Grace to you and peace
from God our Father
and the Lord Jesus Christ. **Amen.**

23 GREETING
Pentecost, ministry, renewal
from 1 Peter 1

Grace and peace be yours in full measure. **Amen.**

24 GREETING
Holy Communion, general
from 1 Peter 5

Peace to all of you who are in Christ:
let us greet one another with love. Amen.

25 GREETING
Invitation to faith, instruction in faith
from 2 Peter 1

Grace and peace be yours in full measure,
through the knowledge of God
and of Jesus our Lord. **Amen.**

26 GREETING
General, word of God
from 2 John

Grace, mercy and peace
from God the Father
and from Jesus Christ, the Father's Son,
be with you in truth and love. **Amen.**

27 GREETING
Holy Communion, family service
from 3 John

Peace to you . . . greet your friends by name. **Amen.**

28 GREETING
Assurance, prayer, elderly
from Jude

You are loved by God the Father
and kept by Jesus Christ:
mercy, peace and love
be yours for ever. **Amen.**

29 GREETING
Advent
from Revelation 1

Grace and peace to you
from him who is, and who was,
and who is to come. **Amen.**

30 GREETING
Easter, All Saints
from Revelation 1

Grace and peace to you
from God who is, who was, and who is to come;
and from Jesus Christ,
the faithful witness,
the first-born from the dead. **Amen.**

31 GREETING
All Saints, Easter
from Revelation 1 (variant)

Grace and peace to you from Jesus Christ,
who is the faithful witness,
the first-born from the dead. **Amen.**

32 GREETING
Unity, people of God
from Revelation 22

The grace of the Lord Jesus be with God's people. **Amen.**

APPROACH

33 APPROACH
Families, commitment
from Deuteronomy 12

Lord, our God,
this is the place where we may worship you;
you have set your name here.
Here in your presence
   our families shall rejoice,
because you have blessed us;
here we present to you
the offering of our lives;
here we pledge our obedience to your laws;
here we pray for our children,
that we and they
   may do what is right in your eyes.
Lord, our God,
this is the place where we may worship you. **Amen.**

34 APPROACH
Church dedication/anniversary, worship
from 1 Kings 8

O Lord our God,
there is no God like you
in heaven above or on earth below:
you keep your covenant of love
with your servants who follow your way
    with all their heart.

You kept your promise to our ancestors –
    with your mouth you promised,
    with your hand you took action!

But will you really live on earth?
The highest heaven cannot contain you:
how much less this house of prayer we have built
    in which to worship you!

Yet, O Lord God, hear our cry,
listen to our plea for mercy;
receive our prayers in your presence today;
let your eyes be open towards this place
which is dedicated/*we now dedicate* to your name.
Hear the intercessions of your people
    when we pray in this place;
hear from heaven
and, when you hear, forgive.

O Lord our God,
there is no God like you! **Amen.**

35 APPROACH
Creation, holidays
from Nehemiah 9

We stand up and praise you, Lord our God,
for you are eternal.
Blest be your glorious name,
exalted above all blessing and praise.
You alone are the Lord;
you made the sky and the stars,
the earth and all that is on it,
the seas and all that is in them;
you give life to everything,
and the hosts of heaven worship you.
We stand up and praise you, Lord our God,
for you are eternal. **Amen.**

36 APPROACH
Morning: penitence, renewal
from Psalm 5

O Lord, our God and king:
in the morning we come to you,
as the sun rises we offer our prayer
and wait for you to answer.
Through your great love
we can come into your house,
we can worship before you
and bow to you in reverence;
but you are not a God
    who is pleased with wrongdoing,
you will allow no evil in your presence –
you cannot tolerate the proud,
and you destroy those
    who live by violence or deceit.
So, lead us to do your will;
make your way plain for us to follow,
help us to find peace in you alone –
to rejoice in you, and sing for joy.
Increase our love for you,
and so make us truly happy;
bless us with obedience to you,
and let your love shield and protect us.
O Lord our God and king,
in the morning we come to you. **Amen.**

37 APPROACH
Deliverance
from Psalm 18

O God, we love you.
We thank you that you are our rock,
our fortress and our deliverer;
we thank you that you are our shield, our might,
and the strength of our salvation.
In our distress we call to you,
we cry to you for help and you listen;
from your holy place you hear our voice.
Our cry comes before you,
it reaches your ears;
and out of heaven
you reach down and take hold of us –
you draw us out of deep waters;
you rescue us from the enemy,
from the foe who is too strong for us.
Therefore we will worship you, O God,
we will sing praises to your name;
for you give us the victory
through our Lord Jesus Christ. **Amen.**

38 APPROACH
Cleansing, expectancy, renewal
from Psalm 24

Lord of the earth and everything in it,
creator of the land and sea:
cleanse our hands and purify our hearts,
that we may stand in your presence and worship you;
keep us from idolatry,
save us from making false promises,
that we may seek your face
and receive your blessing:
for you are the Lord almighty,
the king of glory –
we open the door of our hearts
as you come among us. **Amen.**

39 APPROACH
Holy Communion, church anniversary
from Psalm 26

Lord, thank you for this building
where we come for cleansing,
where we gather round your table,
where we sing aloud your praise,
where we proclaim all you have done for us;
Lord, we love the house
     where you meet us,
the place where your glory dwells:
in the assembly of your people
we stand and praise the Lord! **Amen.**

40 APPROACH
Rededication, commitment, healing
from Psalm 27

Lord, you are our light
   and our salvation;
you protect us from danger,
you remove our fears from us,
you invite us to worship you.
Our greatest desire is to live in your presence:
here we marvel at your goodness
and ask for your guidance;
here, with joyful acclamation,
we offer the sacrifice of our love,
   our gifts and our lives;
here we sing your praise,
here we seek your forgiveness,
here you teach us what you want us to do,
and lead us in safe paths.

We trust you and do not despair:
we know that we will live to see your goodness
   in this present life; ·
and we look to you for the life to come.
Lord, you are our light
   and our salvation. **Amen.**

41 APPROACH
Good Shepherd, dependence on God
from Psalm 28

We praise you, O Lord,
for you hear our cry for mercy;
you are our strength and our shield,
you help us and we trust in you –
our hearts leap for joy,
and we give you thanks in song;
you are the strength of your people:
save us and bless your Church,
be our shepherd –
guide us and guard us for ever. **Amen.**

42 APPROACH
Renewal, Holy Communion
from Psalm 63

O God, you are our God
and we long for you;
with all our being we desire you,
and our spirits are thirsty for you –
we want to sense you in our worship,
we want to feel how mighty and glorious you are.

Because your love is better than life itself,
we will praise you as long as life lasts:
we will give thanks to you;
we will raise our hands to you in prayer,
we will feast upon you and be satisfied.

In the shadow of your wings we sing for joy;
we cling to you,
and you show us your salvation.
O God, you are our God,
and we long for you. **Amen.**

43 APPROACH
Trust, renewal, those in authority
from Psalm 84

Lord almighty,
how we love this place
where we come to worship you;
how we rejoice to be here!
With our whole heart
we sing to you, the living God.

We are happier still
if we always live in your presence,
always singing praises to you:
happy if our strength comes from you,
happy if as we go through life
we are refreshed by the springs of your Spirit,
being strengthened by you on our way,
until we see you face to face.

Lord God almighty,
hear our prayers today
especially for_____/*those in authority.*
You are our protector and glorious king,
blessing us with kindness and honour;
if we do right,
you do not refuse us anything that is good for us.
Lord almighty,
how happy are those who trust in you! **Amen.**

44 APPROACH
People of God, creation, God's majesty
from Psalm 95

Lord, we come to praise you
and to rejoice before you;
you are our defender –
we come before you with thanksgiving,
and sing to you hymns and songs.
You are a mighty God –
king above all gods,
ruling over the heights and depths,
from the deepest hollow to the highest mountain;
ruling over the land and sea
which you yourself have made.

Lord, as we come we bow down before you,
we kneel and worship you – our creator;
for you are our God,
we are your people for whom you care,
your flock for which you provide.

Today, Lord,
we shall listen to what you are saying to us,
for we have seen the wonders you can do. **Amen.**

45 APPROACH (RESPONSIVE)
Justice, God's majesty, Ascensiontide, Trinity
from Psalm 99

Lord, you are king,
and we tremble before you;
you are enthroned in the presence of your people:
let everyone praise
   your great and majestic name –
holy, holy, the Lord our God is holy!

Our mighty king,
you love all that is good;
you bring to us truth and justice –
our Lord God, we praise you
and worship before your throne:
holy, holy, the Lord our God is holy!

Our Lord God,
you answer your people
   when they pray to you;
you speak to us,
and give us your laws to obey;
you show you are a God who forgives –
our Lord God, we praise you,
and come together to worship you:
holy, holy, the Lord our God is holy! Amen.

46 APPROACH
General, creation, rogation, harvest
from Psalm 100

Almighty Lord,
all the earth shouts for joy;
and we your people come before you
  with joyful songs.
We know that you are God;
you made us, and we are yours,
we are your people
  and the sheep of your pasture.
Today we enter your gates with thanksgiving
and come into your presence with praise,
we give thanks to you and praise your name;
for you, Lord, are good,
you are faithful to every generation,
and your love endures for ever and ever. **Amen.**

47 APPROACH
Commitment, Holy Communion, justice
from Psalm 105

O Lord, we thank you for your greatness,
we witness to the wonderful things you have done,
and we are glad that we belong to you.
Today we come to you for strength,
for you are our God;
your justice is for all the world,
your covenant with us is for ever,
and your promises for a thousand generations.
O Lord, we thank you for your greatness. **Amen.**

48 APPROACH
Witness to the world, music, God's love
from Psalm 108

O God, we put our trust in you;
we sing and praise you with all our heart,
our instruments of praise wake up the morning!
we will praise you among those who do not know you,
we will sing to you in front of the world;
for your love is as great as the heavens are high,
and your faithfulness as measureless as the skies:
you show your glory in the heavens,
and your majesty upon earth.
O God, we put our trust in you. **Amen.**

49 APPROACH
Social responsibility, evening
from Psalm 113

Lord,
we come before you now as your servants,
and we worship you:
from sunrise to sunset your name be praised!
You are exalted over all the nations,
your glory fills the skies!
Who is like you, enthroned on high?
Yet you stoop down to look at our world;
you raise up the poor and lift up the needy.
Lord, we come before you now as your servants
and we worship you. **Amen.**

50 APPROACH
Morning: God's love
from Psalm 118

Lord,
this is the day you made;
we rejoice and are glad in it:
save us, prosper us,
bless us as we come into your house;
you have made your light to shine upon us:
we celebrate, and unite to worship you.
You are our God:
we give you thanks, and exalt you.
Lord, you are good,
and your love endures for ever.
Bless us as we come into your house. **Amen.**

51 APPROACH
Families, homes, peace
from Psalm 122

Lord, we rejoiced
when we heard
that we were coming to worship you today;
and now we are here,
standing before you.
To this place of renewal,
of order and harmony,
your people come to give you thanks.

O Lord, bless those who love you;
give us your peace here and in our homes –
peace in our homes
for the sake of our families and friends,
peace here
that your name may be glorified.

Lord, we rejoiced
when we heard
that we were coming to worship you today;
and now we are here,
standing before you. **Amen**

52 APPROACH
Political concern, witness to the world,
  God's word
from Psalm 138

Lord,
we worship you with all our heart;
before the powers of the universe
    we sing your praises.
We come into your house and honour your name
because of your love and faithfulness;
for you have exalted your name and your word
    above all things.
We worship you with all our heart –
    your love endures for ever.
When we called to you, you answered us,
you gave us courage.

Lord,
may the leaders of the nations praise you
when they hear the words of your mouth.
Let them, too, sing of your ways,
for your glory is very great.
Though you are so high,
you look upon the lowly,
but you distance yourself from the proud.
Lord, we worship you with all our heart. **Amen.**

53 APPROACH
Personal devotion, guidance
from Psalm 139

O Lord,
you have searched us and you know us;
you know when we sit down and when we get up;
you see us at work,
you see us at rest,
you know just what we are like.
Before the word is off our lips,
you know what we are going to say.

Lord, you are all around us
and your hand is upon us.
Wherever we go, you are there with us –
your hand guiding us, holding us fast.
However dark it gets, it is not dark to you;
your eyes follow us, you can see us.
For you created us,
formed us before ever we were born –
how wonderfully you made us!
We praise you, Lord:
you know what each day will bring,
and when we wake, you are with us.

O God, you search our hearts,
you lift our anxieties,
you take away our sin,
you lead us in your eternal way;
we praise you, Lord. **Amen.**

54 APPROACH TO GOD
Creation, family, general
from Psalm 148

O God,
we have come to worship you,
the Lord of all creation.
The skies praise you high above,
all the angels praise you – your heavenly army.
The sun, the moon and the shining stars
    all praise you –
they praise your name;
for you commanded and they were created,
you set them in place for ever,
you made a decree that will not pass away.

From the earth
the great sea-creatures praise you,
    in unfathomable ocean depths.
Lightning, hail, snow and clouds – all obey you;
mountains, hills and trees,
wild animals, cattle,
little creatures, birds on the wing – all praise you.

Men, women and children – we too praise you;
here as your people,
holy, and close to your heart – we praise you.
O Lord God, we have come to worship you. **Amen.**

55 APPROACH
Penitence, expectancy, word of God
from Ecclesiastes 5

O God,
we have come to your house;
we tread with guarded steps,
and we draw near to listen.
We do not plead our merit,
for we know we have done wrong:
help us to be silent before you,
to think before we speak.
You are in heaven
and we are on earth;
so we choose our words with care.
Here we make our vows to you:
help us to fulfil them without delay.
Lord, do not let our speech
    lead us into sin;
let us not go back on our promises,
but stand in awe of you,
our judge and our redeemer.
O God,
we have come to your house,
and we draw near to listen. **Amen.**

56 APPROACH
Spring, creation
from Song of Songs 2

See, the winter is past,
the snows are over and gone;
flowers appear on the earth,
the season of singing has come;
the trees are beginning to bud,
the blossom has spread its fragrance;
the cry of the birds is heard in our land:
arise, come and worship. **Amen.**

57 APPROACH

Lent, Advent
from Matthew 24

Lord, we come to you,
the Alpha and Omega,
the beginning and the end.
We wait for your return,
keeping watch because we do not know
  the day or the hour.
We hear of wars and rumours of wars,
and we know that such things must happen –
we know that nation must rise against nation,
that there will be famines and earthquakes,
signs in the sun and the moon,
birth-pangs of the new age:
Yet we also know that all creation
yearns for the freedom of the children of God.

God, as Lord, false prophets appear, *and as conflicting theories attract our attention,*
and we need your discernment.
As The love of many grows cold:
help us to stand firm in our salvation!
Yet the Gospel of the kingdom
  is being preached to the whole world –
as a testimony to every nation;
We see that the leaves of the tree are sprouting
and we know that your summer is near, *though we know neither the day nor the hour.*
For this, O Lord, we *ever* praise you:
knowing that if your heaven and earth will pass away,
but your word stands *will* for ever and ever. **Amen.**

58 APPROACH
Thanksgiving
from Luke 1

Our hearts praise you, O Lord,
our spirits rejoice in God our saviour,
for you have remembered us,
your humble servants.
Mighty God, we celebrate
the great things you have done for us –
your name is holy!
From one generation to another
you have shown mercy on those who honour you.
You have stretched out your mighty arm,
scattering the conceited,
confusing their schemes.
You bring down tyrants
and lift up the lowly;
you fill the hungry with good things,
but send the rich away empty.
You have kept your promises to us;
you have come to our help;
you will show your people your love for ever:
our hearts praise you, O Lord. **Amen.**

59 APPROACH
Holy Communion: evening, especially Easter
from Luke 24

Lord Jesus Christ,
we are your disciples;
it is evening,
the day is nearly over,
and we want you to be with us.
As we open the Scriptures,
talk with us and warm our hearts.
When in your name and at your table
we take bread and give thanks,
when we break it and receive it:
open our eyes, confirm our faith
   and fill us with joy;
that we may believe,
   and declare to all:
'It is true! The Lord has risen.' **Amen.**

60 APPROACH
All Saints, Advent, Holy Communion,
   the church
from Hebrews 12

Come to worship the Lord –
to Mount Zion, to the heavenly Jerusalem,
to the city of the living God,
to thousands upon thousands of angels
   in joyful assembly,
to the church of the first-born,
   whose names are written in heaven;
to God, the judge of all,
to the spirits of the righteous,
to Jesus the mediator of a new covenant.
Do not refuse him who speaks.
Come to worship the Lord! **Amen.**

61 APPROACH
Easter, renewal, heaven
from 1 Peter 1

Praise be to you, our God,
the Father of our Lord Jesus Christ!
In your great mercy
you have given us life and hope
  by raising Jesus Christ from death,
and an inheritance in heaven
  that can never spoil or fade.
Through faith you keep us safe by your power
until the coming salvation
ready to be revealed at the end of time.
For this we praise you through Jesus Christ
whom we love, and in whom we believe,
though we cannot see him;
and our hearts are filled
  with inexpressible and glorious joy
because we are receiving through faith
the salvation of our souls.
Praise be to you, our God! **Amen.**

COMMANDMENT

Advent, Lent, general
from Exodus 20, Deuteronomy 5 and
  New Testament scriptures

'You shall have no other gods but me':
Lord, help us to love you
with all our heart, all our soul,
all our mind and all our strength.

'You shall not make for yourself any idol':
Lord, help us to worship you
in spirit and in truth.

'You shall not dishonour
the name of the Lord your God':
Lord, help us to honour you
with reverence and awe.

'Remember the Lord's day and keep it holy':
Lord, help us to remember Christ
   risen from the dead,
and to set our minds on things above,
not on things on the earth.

'Honour your father and your mother':
Lord, help us to live as your servants,
giving respect to all,
and love to our brothers and sisters in Christ.

'You shall not murder':
Lord, help us to be reconciled with each other,
and to overcome evil with good.

'You shall not commit adultery':
Lord, help us to realize
that our body is a temple of the Holy Spirit.

'You shall not steal':
Lord, help us to be honest in all we do,
and to care for those in need.

'You shall not be a false witness':
Lord, help us always to speak the truth.

'You shall not covet anything
which belongs to your neighbour':
**Lord, help us to remember Jesus said,
'It is more blessed to give than to receive',
and help us to love our neighbours as ourselves;
for his sake. Amen.**

63 COMMANDMENTS: DECLARATION
*Advent, Lent, general
from Exodus 20 and Deuteronomy 5*

**Lord, we will have no other God but you;
we will not make idols for ourselves,
nor will we worship them;
we will not dishonour your name;
we will remember your day and keep it holy;
we will honour our father and our mother;
we will do no murder;
we will not commit adultery;
we will not steal;
we will not be a false witness;
we will not covet anything
    that belongs to another.**

Lord God,
may the awe of your presence
and the vision of your glory
keep us from sinning,
for the sake of Jesus our redeemer. **Amen.**

64 COMMANDMENTS: BEFORE RECITAL
Advent, Lent, general
from Deuteronomy 5

Let us hear the decrees and the laws of the Lord,
learn them, and be sure to follow them: **Amen.**

65 COMMANDMENTS: AFTER RECITAL
Advent, Lent, general
from Deuteronomy 26

You have declared this day
that the Lord is your God,
that you will walk in his ways,
that you will keep his decrees,
commands and laws,
and that you will obey him.
And the Lord declares this day
that you are his people,
his treasured possession;
a people holy to the Lord your God,
as he promised in Jesus Christ our Saviour.
Thanks be to God. Amen.

66 COMMANDMENTS: CONFESSION
Holy Communion, general
from Mark 12
see also numbers 70, 80 and 82

Jesus said:
Love the Lord your God
with all your heart and with all your soul
and with all your mind and with all your strength;
and love your neighbour as yourself.
Lord, we have broken your commandments;
forgive us, and help us to obey;
for your name's sake. **Amen.**

67 COMMANDMENTS: DECLARATION
Advent, social responsibility, general
from Mark 12

Our Lord God,
you are the only Lord;
and we will love you
with all our heart
and with all our soul
and with all our mind
and with all our strength;
and we will love our neighbours
   as ourselves:
Lord help us to obey your commandments
and so be ready for the kingdom of God;
through Jesus our redeemer. **Amen.**

68 COMMANDMENTS: PRAYER
Holy Communion, Advent, Lent,
  social responsibility
from Romans 13

The commandments:
do not commit adultery,
do not commit murder,
do not steal,
do not desire what belongs to another –
these and all others
are summed up in one command:
love your neighbour as you love yourself:
Lord, help us to love our neighbours,
and to do them no wrong,
so that we may obey your law. Amen.

CONFESSION

69 CONFESSION
People of God, general
from Exodus 34

Lord, the only God,
compassionate and gracious,
slow to anger and full of love:
be with us now.
Judge of the guilty,
we have been stubborn,
we have rebelled against you:
forgive our wickedness and sin,
and receive us as your own;
though Jesus Christ our Lord. **Amen**.

70 CONFESSION
God's word to us, after commandments
from 2 Kings 22

Lord, we have not obeyed your word,
nor heeded
   what is written in the Scriptures:
we repent with all our heart,
and humble ourselves before you.
In your mercy forgive us;
grant us your peace
and the strength to keep your laws;
through Jesus Christ our Lord. **Amen**.

71 CONFESSION
Guilt, general
from Ezra 9

O God,
we are too ashamed and disgraced
to lift up our faces to you,
because our sins are higher than our heads,
and our guilt has reached you in heaven.
O Lord, you are righteous;
we bow before you in our guiltiness,
not one of us can stand in your presence.
Forgive us; in Jesus' name. **Amen**.

72 CONFESSION
Commandments, general
from Nehemiah 9

Our Lord God,
great, mighty and awesome,
gracious and merciful:
you keep your covenant of love;
you have acted faithfully,
    while we have done wrong;
we did not follow your commandments
or pay attention to the warnings you gave us;
even while we were enjoying your great goodness
we did not serve you,
or turn from our evil ways.
Because of our sin
    our happiness is taken away –
our enemy rules over our souls and bodies,
and we are in great distress:
forgive us and restore us
for your name's sake. **Amen**.

73 CONFESSION
Majesty of God, general
from Job 40–42

Lord, you are without equal,
everything in creation is yours:
we are unworthy
and have to answer to you.
We confess our lack of understanding
and repent of all our sin.
Lord, our ears have heard of you,
and now our eyes have seen you:
forgive us; through Jesus our redeemer. **Amen**.

74 CONFESSION
Civic, social responsibility, general
from Psalm 15

Lord God,
we are not worthy to come before you,
or to live in your presence,
for we are to blame for our failure to do right:
we have not always spoken the truth
    from our heart,
nor has our tongue been free from slander;
we have wronged our friends
and criticized our neighbours;
we have condoned evil,
and not honoured those who fear you;
we have not kept our promises
    when it hurt us to do so;
we have not used our wealth to your glory:
O Lord, forgive us and help us;
for your name's sake. **Amen**.

75 CONFESSION
Social responsibility
from Psalm 41

Lord, have mercy on us,
for we have sinned against you:
we have failed to care for the weak,
and have fallen into sin.
O Lord, have mercy on us
and raise us up;
uphold us in the truth
and keep us in your presence for ever;
for Jesus' sake. **Amen**.

76 CONFESSION
Renewal, general
from Psalm 51

Lord God, have mercy on us,
according to your steadfast love;
and in your abundant mercy,
blot out our transgressions:
cleanse us from our sin,
create in us a clean heart and life,
and continually renew
a right spirit within us. **Amen**.

77 CONFESSION
General
from Psalm 51 (alternative)

O God,
in your goodness have mercy on us,
wash us clean from our guilt
and purify us from our sin.
We know our faults well,
and our sins hang heavy upon us.
Against you only have we sinned
and done evil in your sight;
so you are right to judge us,
you are justified in condemning us:
remove our sin, and we will be clean;
wash us, and we will be whiter than snow;
hide your face from our sins,
and wipe out all our guilt;
through Jesus Christ our Lord. **Amen.**

78 CONFESSION
National and church repentance
from Psalm 79

O God,
we are being punished for our sins,
and those who do not worship you have benefited:
do not be angry with us for ever,
have mercy on us now,
help us and save us,
rescue us and forgive our sins;
for your name's sake. **Amen.**

79 CONFESSION
Morning, pride, ministry
from Psalm 101

Lord God,
our hearts are guilty;
   we have been dishonest,
   we have looked on evil,
   we have clung to our selfish ways,
   we have talked about others behind their backs –
   with haughty eyes and a proud heart.
Lord, forgive us and help us;
renew us in righteousness every morning,
make our lives faithful
and our speech blameless,
that we may live in your presence for ever;
through Jesus Christ our Lord. **Amen**.

80 CONFESSION
After commandments, general
from Psalm 106

O Lord our God,
we have not obeyed your commands,
we have not always done what is right;
we have sinned in the weakness of our fallen humanity,
we have done wrong and acted wickedly;
we have forgotten your many kindnesses
and we have rebelled against you:
O Lord, forgive us and save us,
bring us back and restore us;
that we may give thanks to your holy name
and glorify you in our worship. **Amen**.

81 CONFESSION
Evening, heaven, general
from Psalm 109

Lord, we need you;
our hearts are wounded,
our days fade like evening shadows,
we are weak and despise ourselves;
for we have sinned against you:
forgive us, O Lord,
and in your constant love save us;
through Jesus our redeemer. **Amen**.

82 CONFESSION
After commandments, general
from Psalm 119 (1–8)

Lord, we are to blame,
for we have not followed your law –
we have not kept your commandments,
we have not sought for you with all our heart,
we have not walked in your ways,
nor have we fully obeyed you.
Lord, we long to be faithful and obedient:
do not put us to shame.
Give us upright hearts,
teach us obedience
and do not forsake us for ever. **Amen**.

83 CONFESSION
Invitation to faith, general
from Psalm 130

Lord, we cry to you
　　from the depths of our being:
let your ears be open
　　as we plead for mercy.
If you kept a record of our sins
none of us could stand before you;
but you alone can forgive us,
therefore we come to you in awe.
Lord, we wait for you –
and in your promise we put our hope;
through our saviour Jesus Christ. **Amen.**

84 CONFESSION
Lent, temptation, general
from Psalm 142

Lord, we have sinned:
we lift up our voice to you
and cry for your mercy.
There is no one else to whom we can go:
save us from our sins
and from temptations that are too strong for us.
Set us free,
that we may praise your name;
through Jesus Christ our Lord. **Amen.**

85 CONFESSION

In time of trouble, renewal,
* evening, general*
from Psalm 143

Lord, we have failed you:
darkness overtakes us,
our spirits tremble
and our hearts are dismayed;
your face is hidden from us
and we wait for your word of love.
Hear our prayer,
listen to our cry for mercy;
in your faithfulness and righteousness
come to our relief.
Do not bring us to judgement –
for no one living is righteous before you;
show us the way we should go,
teach us to do your will
and let your Spirit lead us;
through Jesus Christ our Lord. **Amen.**

86 CONFESSION

Trinity, majesty of God, repentance, ministry
from Isaiah 6

Lord our God,
enthroned on high,
filling the whole earth with your glory:
holy, holy, holy is your name.
Our eyes have seen the King,
the Lord almighty;
but our lips are unclean.
We cry to you in our sinfulness
to take our guilt away,
through Jesus Christ our Lord. **Amen.**

87 CONFESSION
Civic, national, stewardship
from Isaiah 43

Lord our God,
we confess that we have not prayed to you,
nor have we tried hard to serve you;
we have not given to you from our wealth,
nor have we honoured you
  with the work of our hands;
but we have burdened you with our sins,
and wearied you with our wrongdoing:
blot out our transgressions
and remember our sin no more,
for your name's sake. **Amen.**

88 CONFESSION
General, national, renewal
from Isaiah 57

Lord God,
you are eternal, and your name is holy;
you live in a high and holy place –
yet also with the humble and penitent:
revive our spirits,
renew our hearts;
do not accuse us
or be angry with us for ever.

We confess our selfishness
and our wilful ways;
you have punished us,
you have hidden your face from us:
Lord God, forgive us;
through Jesus our redeemer. **Amen.**

89 CONFESSION
General, civic, national
from Isaiah 59

Lord God,
our offences are many in your sight,
and our failures testify against us;
our wrongdoing is ever with us,
and we acknowledge our sin;
we have rebelled against you
and acted treacherously towards you,
turning our backs on you:
Lord God, forgive us;
through Jesus our redeemer. **Amen.**

90 CONFESSION
Lent, general
from Isaiah 63

God, our Father,
we have strayed from your ways;
we have been stubborn
and have turned away from you.
You are the one who has always rescued us:
look upon us from heaven
    where you live in holiness and glory;
show your love for us,
show your power,
show your mercy.
For our sake, who love you –
for our sake, who are your people,
return to us and forgive;
through Jesus Christ our Lord. **Amen.**

91 CONFESSION
Renewal, general
from Isaiah 64

Sovereign Lord,
we have sinned continually against you;
we have become unclean,
all our righteous acts are like filthy rags;
we shrivel up like leaves,
and our sins sweep us away.
Yet, O Lord, you are our Father:
do not remember our sins for ever.
We are your people:
look upon us, we pray,
and forgive us;
through Jesus our redeemer. **Amen.**

92 CONFESSION
National, social responsibility
from Jeremiah 14

Lord,
we acknowledge our own wickedness
and the guilt of our society;
we have sinned against you.
For the sake of your name,
   do not despise us;
remember your covenant in Jesus our redeemer,
and forgive us our sin;
for his name's sake. **Amen.**

93 CONFESSION
New Year, general
from Lamentations 5

Lord,
remember your people in their sorrow;
look, and see our disgrace:
joy has gone from our hearts,
our dancing has turned to mourning;
we are no longer proud,
for we have sinned.
You, Lord, reign for ever;
your throne endures to every generation:
do not forget us now,
do not forsake us for long –
forgive us, restore us and renew us;
through Jesus our redeemer. **Amen.**

94 CONFESSION
People of God, national, God's word
from Daniel 9

Let us pray to the Lord our God
and confess the sins of his people:

Lord, you are great
and we honour you;
you are faithful to us,
and show your constant love
**   to those who love you,**
**   and do what you command:**
we have sinned and done wrong,
we have been wicked,
we have rebelled,
we have turned away from your commandments
**   and your laws,**
we have not listened to your voice.

Lord, you are righteous –
but today we are ashamed,
because we have sinned against you:
O Lord, listen,
O Lord, hear,
O Lord, forgive;
for your name's sake. Amen.

95 CONFESSION
Unity, general
from Daniel 9

Lord our God,
you brought your people out of slavery
with a mighty hand,
and made for yourself
a name which endures to this day:

We have sinned, we have done wrong.
O Lord, hear:
O Lord, forgive!

In keeping with all your righteous acts,
turn away your anger from your people.
O Lord, hear:
O Lord, forgive!

Our sins have made us despised
    by those around us.
O Lord, hear:
O Lord, forgive!

We do not come before you
because we are righteous,
but because of your great mercy.
O Lord, hear:
O Lord, forgive! Amen.

96 CONFESSION
Repentance after failure
from Hosea 14

O Lord our God,
our sins have been our downfall,
but now we turn to you
and confess them:
forgive us our sins
and receive our prayer
that we may praise you once again;
through Jesus Christ our Lord. **Amen**.

97 CONFESSION
Sea theme, general
from Jonah 2

Lord God,
in our distress we call to you;
from the depths we cry for help.
The storm swirls around us,
our troubles threaten to engulf us,
we feel we have been banished from your sight;
but we look again for your love and peace.

We have clung to worthless things
and forfeited the grace
    that could have been ours;
we are trapped under a weight of sin,
and our life is ebbing away.
O Lord, we call to you:
forgive us and restore us;
through Jesus Christ our Saviour. **Amen**.

98 CONFESSION
Faith, evangelism, general
from Acts 3

God our Father,
you have given your divine glory,
to your servant Jesus,
   holy and good,
the one who leads to life;
but we have betrayed and rejected him:
now we repent and turn to you again,
that you might forgive our sins
and strengthen us
by sending into our hearts
your holy Spirit;
through Jesus Christ our Lord. **Amen.**

99 CONFESSION
Invitation to faith, general
from 1 John 1

God our Father,
if we say that we have no sin,
   we deceive ourselves,
and the truth is not in us:
if we confess our sins,
you will keep your promise
and do what is right –
you will forgive us our sins,
and cleanse us from every kind of wrong:
Father, have mercy on us;
through Jesus Christ our Lord. **Amen.**

100 CONFESSION
Invitation to faith, general
from 1 John 1 (alternative)

Lord God,
you have taught us
that if we say we have no sin
we deceive ourselves
and the truth is not in us:
we humbly confess our sins to you.
Now keep your promise:
forgive us our sins,
and cleanse us from all unrighteousness;
through Jesus Christ our Lord. **Amen.**

DECLARATION OF FORGIVENESS
ABSOLUTION

101 ABSOLUTION

Renewal, God's love to us
from Ezra 9

The Lord *your* God is gracious:
he surrounds *you* with his love,
gives light to *your* eyes
and freedom from *your* sins.
God has not deserted *you* –
he shows *you* kindness and grants *you* new life;
in Christ Jesus our Lord. **Amen.**

102 ABSOLUTION

Repentance, general
from Nehemiah 9

The Lord our God is a forgiving God,
gracious and merciful,
slow to anger and full of love;
because of his great compassion
he will not abandon us.
You were disobedient and rebelled against him,
yet from heaven he hears *you* in *your* distress,
he forgives *your* sin and delivers *you*;
through Jesus Christ our Lord. **Amen.**

103 ABSOLUTION

Healing, general
from Psalm 6

The Lord God be merciful to *you* and heal *you*;
the Lord turn his face towards *you* and deliver *you*;
the Lord save *you* in his unfailing love;
through Jesus Christ our Lord. **Amen.**

104 ABSOLUTION
Passiontide, renewal, general
from Psalm 6

The Lord God, who sees *your* sorrow
and hears *your* weeping;
receives *your* cry for mercy
and accepts *your* prayer;
through Jesus Christ our redeemer. **Amen.**

105 ABSOLUTION
Good Shepherd, Rogation, general
from Psalm 28

Praise the Lord,
for he has heard your cry for mercy:
in Christ you are forgiven,
he is your strength and shield –
trust in him and he will help you.
Rejoice and give thanks to him in song,
for he is the strength of his people
and will be your salvation.
He will save you and bless you;
he will be your Shepherd
and care for you for ever. **Amen.**

106 ABSOLUTION
Good Shepherd, Rogation, general
from Psalm 28 (alternative)

Let us praise the Lord,
for he has heard our cry for mercy:
in Christ we are forgiven,
he is our strength and shield –
let us trust in him and he will help us.
Let us rejoice and thank him in song,
for he is the strength of his people
and will be our salvation.
He will save us and bless us;
he will be our Shepherd
and care for us for ever. **Amen.**

107 ABSOLUTION
Temptation, Lent, general
from Psalm 31

The Lord have mercy upon *you* in *your* distress;
the Lord deliver *you* from *your* sins
and shelter *you* in all temptation;
the Lord make his face to shine upon *you*,
and save *you* in his unfailing love. **Amen.**

108 ABSOLUTION
Majesty of God, general
from Psalm 32

You are blessed by the Lord:
your sins are forgiven,
    your faults are covered;
the Lord will not count your sin against you,
for you have confessed to him
and have not deceived him:
rejoice in the Lord and be glad! **Amen.**

109 ABSOLUTION
Majesty of God, general
from Psalm 32 (alternative)

We are blessed by the Lord:
our sins are forgiven,
    our faults are covered;
he will not count our sins against us,
for we have confessed to the Lord
and have not deceived him:
let us rejoice in the Lord and be glad. **Amen.**

110 ABSOLUTION
Renewal, invitation to faith, general
from Psalm 51

God in his goodness have mercy on *you*,
wash *you* clean from *your* guilt
and purify *you* from *your* sin;
God the righteous judge
remove *your* sins from *you*,
and make *you* whiter than snow;
through Jesus Christ our saviour. **Amen.**

111 ABSOLUTION
Lent, faith, general
from Psalm 51

The Lord God have mercy on *you*
according to his steadfast love,
and in his abundant mercy
blot out *your* transgressions;
the Lord cleanse *you* from *your* sin,
create in *you* a clean heart and life,
and continually renew a right spirit within *you*;
for Jesus' sake. **Amen.**

112 ABSOLUTION
Lent, faith, general
from Psalm 51 (variant)

The Lord has mercy on *you*
according to his steadfast love,
in his abundant mercy
he blots out *your* transgressions
and cleanses *you* from *your* sin;
through Jesus *your* redeemer. **Amen.**

113 ABSOLUTION
Invitation to faith, renewal, general
from Psalm 51

God, the righteous judge,
removes *your* sins from *you*
and washes *you* whiter than snow;
may he give *you* a pure heart,
may he strengthen *you* and renew *your* spirit,
may he restore to *you* his presence
and bring *you* the joy of his salvation;
through Jesus Christ our Lord. **Amen.**

114 ABSOLUTION
Pentecost, renewal, general
from Psalm 51

The Lord hide his face from *your* sins
and blot out all *your* iniquity;
the Lord create in *you* a pure heart,
and renew within *you* a strong spirit;
the Lord give you again
    the joy that comes from his salvation
and make you willing to obey him;
through Jesus our redeemer. **Amen.**

115 ABSOLUTION
Holiness of God, general
from Psalm 99

The Lord your God
answers your prayer
and forgives your sin:
praise the Lord your God
for he is holy! **Amen.**

116 ABSOLUTION
Holiness of God, general
from Psalm 99 (alternative)

May the Lord our God
answer our prayers
and forgive our sin:
let us praise the Lord our God
for he is holy! **Amen.**

117 ABSOLUTION
After Easter, general
from Psalm 103

The Lord forgive *you* all *your* sins,
and heal the disease of *your* soul;
the Lord redeem *your life* from the grave,
and bless *you* with his love and mercy. **Amen.**

118 ABSOLUTION
After Easter, general
from Psalm 103 (variant)

The Lord forgives *you* all *your* sins,
and heals the disease of *your* soul;
the Lord redeems *your life* from the grave,
and blesses *you* with his love and mercy. **Amen.**

119 ABSOLUTION
Creation, invitation to faith, general
from Psalm 103

God who is merciful and loving
will not punish *you* as *you* deserve,
nor repay *you* for *your* sins and wrongdoing.
As high as the sky is above the earth,
so great is his love for *you*;
as far as the east is from the west,
so far has he removed *your* sins from *you*;
through Jesus Christ our Lord. **Amen.**

120 ABSOLUTION
God's love for us, general
from Psalm 103

The Lord,
merciful and gracious,
slow to be angry and full of love,
will not accuse *you* for ever,
or be angry with *you* always;
he does not treat *you* as *your* sins deserve,
nor repay *you* according to *your* wrongdoing:
he has compassion on *you*
as a father has compassion on his children,
and forgives *you your* sins;
through Jesus Christ our Lord. **Amen.**

121 ABSOLUTION
God's love for us, general
from Psalm 103 (alternative)

The Lord,
who is merciful and gracious,
slow to be angry and full of love;
who will not accuse us for ever,
or be angry with us always;
who does not treat us as our sins deserve,
or repay us according to our wrongdoing:
have compassion on *you*
as a father has compassion on his children,
and forgive *you your* sins;
through Jesus Christ our Lord. **Amen.**

122 ABSOLUTION
Creation, invitation to faith, general
from Psalm 103 (variant)

The Lord,
whose love for those who seek him
is as great
as the heavens are high above the earth,
removes *your* sins from *you*
as far as the east is from the west,
and will remember them no more;
through Jesus Christ our Lord. **Amen.**

123 ABSOLUTION
In anxiety, general
from Psalm 116

The Lord knows your voice,
the Lord hears your cry for mercy,
the Lord turns his ear toward you;
the Lord is gracious and righteous,
he is full of compassion.
In your need he has saved you.
Be at peace – God forgives you. **Amen.**

124 ABSOLUTION
In anxiety, general
from Psalm 116 (alternative)

The Lord knows our voice,
the Lord hears our cry for mercy,
the Lord turns his ear towards us;
the Lord is gracious and righteous,
he is full of compassion;
in our need he has saved us.
Let us be at peace –
God has forgiven us. **Amen.**

125 ABSOLUTION
Evil, temptation, God's love
from Psalm 118

The Lord is good – his love endures for ever;
the Lord is with you:
do not be afraid!
He hears the cry of your heart,
and sets you free from your sins.
Your enemy is cut off from you;
you will not die, but live
and proclaim what the Lord has done. **Amen.**

126 ABSOLUTION
Evil, temptation, God's love
from Psalm 118 (alternative)

The Lord is good – his love endures for ever;
the Lord is with us:
let us not be afraid!
He hears the cry of our hearts
and sets us free from our sins.
Our enemy is cut off from us;
we shall not die, but live
and proclaim what the Lord has done. **Amen.**

127 ABSOLUTION
Discipleship, general
from Psalm 119 (25–32)

The Lord restores your life
as he has promised,
for *you* have confessed what *you* have done:
the Lord has heard *you* and forgiven *you*.

The Lord in his goodness teach *you* his ways,
the Lord strengthen *you*,
the Lord keep *you* from going the wrong way,
and from being put to shame;
the Lord make *you* eager to obey his commands,
and give *you* understanding. **Amen.**

128 ABSOLUTION
Lent, temptation, general
from Psalm 119 (129–136)

God,
who has mercy on those who love him,
turn to you and forgive you
    as he has promised;
keep you from falling,
preserve you from all evil,
bless you with his presence
and teach you his commandments;
through Jesus Christ our saviour. **Amen.**

129 ABSOLUTION
Passiontide, general
from Psalm 130

People of God,
trust the Lord:
the Lord's love never fails,
and he saves utterly.
The Lord himself
redeems/*will redeem* you from all your sins;
through our Saviour, Jesus Christ. **Amen.**

130 ABSOLUTION
Passiontide, general
from Psalm 130 (alternative)

People of God,
let us put our hope in the Lord:
for with the Lord is unfailing love,
with him there is full redemption.
The Lord himself
redeems/*will redeem* us from all our sins;
through our Saviour, Jesus Christ. **Amen.**

131 ABSOLUTION
Protection, general
from Psalm 140

The Lord *your* God hears *your* cry for mercy;
you shall not die,
for the Sovereign Lord, *your* strong deliverer,
is *your* helmet of salvation
through Jesus Christ our Lord. **Amen.**

132 ABSOLUTION
Protection and provision
from Psalm 142

The Lord hears *your* cry
and gives *you* his mercy;
he watches over *you* and sees *your* trouble;
he is *your* refuge
and the hope of *your* life –
he knows *your* need;
in Jesus Christ he sets *you* free,
so that *you* may praise his name. **Amen.**

133 ABSOLUTION
God as carer/parent
from Psalm 145

God is gracious and compassionate,
slow to anger and rich in love;
he loves *you*
and keeps his promise to forgive *you*;
he lifts *you* up and hears *your* cry and saves *you*;
through Jesus Christ our Lord. **Amen.**

134 ABSOLUTION
Forgiveness through Christ
from Isaiah 12

Praise the Lord:
although he was angry with you,
in the name of Jesus
  his anger is turned away.
The Lord comforts you;
he is your salvation –
trust, and do not be afraid. **Amen.**

135 ABSOLUTION
Forgiveness through Christ
from Isaiah 12 (alternative)

Praise the Lord:
although he was angry with us,
for the sake of Jesus
  his anger is turned away.
The Lord comforts us;
he is our salvation:
let us trust him, and not be afraid. **Amen.**

136 ABSOLUTION
Comfort
from Isaiah 25

The faithful Lord, the sovereign Lord,
wipes away your tears
and removes your disgrace from you.
The Lord has spoken –
he is your God:
trust him and he will save you,
rejoice and be glad in his redemption;
through Christ Jesus. **Amen.**

137 ABSOLUTION
Comfort
from Isaiah 25 (alternative)

The faithful Lord, the sovereign Lord,
wipes away our tears
and removes our disgrace from us.
The Lord has spoken –
he is our God:
let us trust him and he will save us,
let us rejoice and be glad in his redemption;
through Christ Jesus. **Amen.**

138 ABSOLUTION
Invitation to faith, general
from Isaiah 38

The Lord restore *your* health,
the Lord bring *you* salvation
and let *you* live;
the Lord in his love keep *you*
    from [the pit of] destruction
and put *your* sins
    behind his back for ever. **Amen.**

139 ABSOLUTION
Advent, Christmas, people of God
from Isaiah 40

Hear God's tender words of comfort for his people:
'Your struggles are ended, your sin is paid for'.

God will show you his glory,
and you will receive the grace of forgiveness
    at his hand;
through Jesus Christ our Lord. **Amen.**

140 ABSOLUTION
Advent, Christmas, people of God
from Isaiah 40 (alternative)

Hear God's tender words of comfort for his people:
'Your struggles are ended, your sin is paid for'.

God will show us his glory:
and we shall receive the grace of forgiveness
   at his hand;
through Jesus Christ our Lord. **Amen.**

141 ABSOLUTION
Encouragement, strengthening,
   people of God
from Isaiah 41

Receive forgiveness in the name of our God.
You are his servant –
he has chosen you and has not rejected you:
do not fear, for he is with you;
do not be dismayed, for he is your God –
he will strengthen you and help you;
he will uphold you with his righteous right hand;
through Jesus Christ our Lord. **Amen.**

142 ABSOLUTION
Encouragement, strengthening,
  people of God
from Isaiah 41 (alternative)

Let us receive forgiveness in the name of our God.

We are his servants,
he has chosen us and not rejected us:
let us not fear, for he is with us,
nor be afraid, for he is our God –
he will strengthen us and help us;
he will uphold us with his righteous right hand;
through Jesus Christ our Lord. **Amen.**

143 ABSOLUTION
Faith, penitence, general
from Isaiah 43

The Lord, *your* redeemer, the Holy One,
blot out *your* transgressions
and remember *your* sins no more;
for his name's sake. **Amen.**

144 ABSOLUTION
Faith, penitence, general
from Isaiah 43 (alternative)

The Lord, *your* redeemer, the Holy One,
blots out *your* transgressions
and remembers *your* sins no more;
for his name's sake. **Amen.**

145 ABSOLUTION
Faith, penitence, general
from Isaiah 43 (variant)

This is what the Lord says –
your redeemer, the Holy One:
'I, even I, will blot out your transgressions,
and remember your sins no more;
for my name's sake.' **Amen.**

146 ABSOLUTION
Ministry, assurance, general
from Isaiah 49

Hear the assurance of God's forgiveness:

In the time of his favour the Lord answers you;
in the day of salvation he helps you;
the Lord comforts you,
he has compassion upon you;
he has not forsaken you,
nor has he forgotten you.
Lift up your eyes and look around:
the Lord is your saviour
and your redeemer;
in Christ you are forgiven. **Amen.**

147 ABSOLUTION
Ministry, assurance, general
from Isaiah 49 (alternative)

Let us hear the assurance of God's forgiveness:

'In the time of salvation the Lord answers you;
in the day of salvation he helps you;
the Lord comforts you,
he has compassion upon you.'
Let us lift up our eyes and look around:
the Lord is our saviour
and our redeemer;
in Christ we are forgiven. **Amen.**

148 ABSOLUTION
Good Friday, Passiontide
from Isaiah 53

Receive God's forgiveness
   through our Lord Jesus Christ:
he covers your weaknesses
and carries your sorrows;
he was pierced for your transgressions
and crushed for your iniquities;
he took your punishment upon himself
   to bring you peace:
by his wounds you are healed. **Amen.**

149 ABSOLUTION
Good Friday, Passiontide
from Isaiah 53 (alternative)

Let us receive God's forgiveness
    through our Lord Jesus Christ:
he covers our weaknesses
and carries our sorrows;
he was pierced for our transgressions
and crushed for our iniquities;
he took our punishment upon himself
    to bring us peace:
by his wounds we are healed. **Amen.**

150 ABSOLUTION
Ministry, prayer, general
from Isaiah 59

The arm of God is not too short to save,
nor his ear too dull to hear:
the Lord our redeemer comes to us
when we repent of our sins:
in the name of Jesus *your* sins are forgiven;
God's Spirit and his word will not leave *you*
from this time on for ever. **Amen.**

151 ABSOLUTION
Ministry of God, renewal, general
from Lamentations 5

The Lord who reigns for ever,
whose throne endures from generation to generation,
has not forgotten *you*,
nor has he forsaken *you*:
he forgives the sins *you* have confessed to him.
The Lord will restore *you* to himself
and renew *your* days;
through our saviour Jesus Christ. **Amen.**

152 ABSOLUTION
Discipleship, God's love, general
from Hosea 14

The Lord heals your waywardness
and loves you freely;
he is no longer angry with you,
and forgives you;
through our Lord Jesus Christ. **Amen.**

153 ABSOLUTION
Prayer, healing, general
from Jonah 2

Because you have remembered the Lord your God
he listens to your prayer,
he hears your cry and he answers you;
he brings up your life from the depths,
he forgives all your sin:
praise him with a song of thanksgiving,
make good your promises to him.
Salvation comes from the Lord! **Amen.**

154 ABSOLUTION
Prayer, healing, general
from Jonah 2 (alternative)

Because we have remembered the Lord our God
he listens to our prayer,
he hears our cry and answers us;
he brings us up from the depths,
he forgives all our sins:
let us praise him with songs of thanksgiving
and make good our promises to him.
Salvation comes from the Lord! **Amen.**

155 ABSOLUTION
Moral failure, general
from John 8 and Romans 8

Jesus said,
'I do not condemn you: go and sin no more'.
There is no more condemnation
for those who are in Christ Jesus. **Amen.**

156 ABSOLUTION
Pentecost, baptism renewal
from 1 Corinthians 6

Now you are washed,
you are sanctified,
you are justified;
in the name of the Lord Jesus
and by the Spirit of our God. **Amen.**

157 ABSOLUTION
Confirmation, assurance, general
from Ephesians 2

You, who once were far away,
have been brought near through the blood of Christ:
he himself is your peace. **Amen.**

158 ABSOLUTION
All Saints, faith, general
from Colossians 1

God has rescued you from the power of darkness,
and brought you safe
into the kingdom of his dear Son:
in Christ *your* sins are forgiven
and *you* are set free. **Amen.**

159 ABSOLUTION
Faith, guilt, Passiontide
from Hebrews 10

Draw near
with a sincere heart and a sure faith:
you are purged from your guilt
and washed clean through the blood of Christ.
Hold on to this hope,
and trust the promises of God. **Amen.**

160 ABSOLUTION
Faith, guilt, Passiontide
from Hebrews 10 (alternative)

Let us draw near
with a sincere heart and a sure faith:
we are purged from our guilt
and washed clean through the blood of Christ.
Let us hold on to this hope,
and trust the promises of God. **Amen.**

161 ABSOLUTION
General
from 1 John 2

[Hear the word of the Lord:]

My child,
your sins are forgiven
for the sake of Christ. **Amen.**

162 ABSOLUTION
Love of God, Holy Communion, general
from 1 John 4

Because God loves *you*,
and by means of his Son
whom God sent,
your sins are forgiven. **Amen.**

EXHORTATION

163 EXHORTATION
Ascension, general
from Exodus 15

Let us sing to the Lord our God,
majestic in holiness,
awesome in glory,
working wonders:
for he is highly exalted and he will reign
for ever and ever. **Amen.**

164 EXHORTATION
God's people, Holy Communion, celebration,
*   anniversary*
from Psalm 30

Sing praise to the Lord,
all his faithful people;
remember what the Holy One has done
and give him thanks! **Amen.**

165 EXHORTATION
Ministry, unity
from Psalm 34

Glorify the Lord with me:
let us praise his name together. Amen.

166 EXHORTATION
Epiphany, Rogation, creation
from Psalm 66

Shout with joy to God, all the earth,
sing to the glory of his name;
come and see what God has done,
how awesome are his works!
Praise our God, all you people,
sound aloud his praise! **Amen.**

167 EXHORTATION
God's people, mission
from Psalm 72

Praise the Lord, the God of Israel –
he alone does marvellous things;
praise his glorious name for ever,
let his praises fill the earth! **Amen.**

168 EXHORTATION
Harvest, general
from Psalm 95

Come, let us sing for joy to the Lord,
let us shout to the Rock of our salvation,
let us come before him with thanksgiving,
and sing him joyful songs of praise! **Amen.**

169 EXHORTATION
Harvest, general
from Psalm 95 (variant)

Come, let us sing for joy to the Lord;
let us come before him with thanksgiving,
and extol him with music and song. **Amen.**

170 EXHORTATION
Palm Sunday, Ascension, general
from Psalm 95

Come, let us bow down in worship;
let us kneel before the Lord our maker. **Amen.**

171 EXHORTATION
Easter, Ascension, musical occasion, general
from Psalm 96

Sing a new song to the Lord;
sing to the Lord and praise his name,
proclaim his triumph day by day! **Amen.**

172 EXHORTATION
Epiphany, Trinity, holiness, general
from Psalm 96

Worship the Lord in the splendour of his holiness;
tremble before him, all the earth:
great is the Lord, and worthy to be praised. Amen.

173 EXHORTATION
Epiphany, worldwide church, mission
from Psalm 98

Sing to the Lord, all the world,
for the Lord is a mighty God;
sing a new song to the Lord,
for he has done marvellous things;
proclaim his glory among the nations,
and shout for joy to the Lord our king! **Amen.**

174 EXHORTATION
General
from Psalm 98 (variant)

Sing to the Lord a new song,
for he has done marvellous things;
sing for joy to the Lord, all the earth,
praise him with songs and shouts of joy! **Amen.**

175 EXHORTATION
Celebration, thanksgiving, mission, service
from Psalm 100

Shout for joy to the Lord, all the earth,
serve him with gladness;
come before him with joyful songs,
give thanks to him and praise his name! **Amen.**

176 EXHORTATION
Healing, forgiveness, God's love and providence
from Psalm 103

Praise the Lord,
and do not forget his blessings.
He forgives your sins
   and heals your diseases;
he crowns you with his love
and satisfies your need.
Praise the Lord! **Amen.**

177 EXHORTATION
General
from Psalm 105

Give thanks to the Lord, call on his name;
make his deeds known in the world around.
Sing to him, sing praise to him;
tell of the wonderful things he has done.
Glory in his holy name;
let those who seek the Lord rejoice! **Amen.**

178 EXHORTATION
Trinity, God's love, general
from Psalm 106

Give thanks to the Lord, for he is good:
his love endures for ever.
Tell of all his mighty acts,
and make his praises heard.
Praise be to the Lord, the God of Israel,
from everlasting to everlasting!
Let all the people say, 'Amen':
Praise the Lord! **Amen.**

179 EXHORTATION
God's love and faithfulness
from Psalm 107

Let us give thanks to God,
for he is good
and his love endures for ever. **Amen.**

180 EXHORTATION
Passiontide, God's love, faith
from Psalm 107

The Lord has redeemed us:
let us thank him for his love
and the wonderful things he has done. **Amen.**

181 EXHORTATION
God's love and faithfulness
from Psalm 107 (variant)

Let us give thanks to the Lord
for his unfailing love. **Amen.**

182 EXHORTATION
Thanksgiving, general
from Psalm 107 (variant)

Let us give thanks to the Lord
   for his unfailing love
and the wonders he has done for us. **Amen.**

183 EXHORTATION
Dedication, general
from Psalm 113

Praise the Lord, you servants of the Lord;
praise the name of the Lord. **Amen.**

184 EXHORTATION
Evening, ministers, choir
from Psalm 134

All of you who serve the Lord,
who come in the evening of the day
to worship in his house:
lift up your hands in this holy place
and praise the Lord.
[And the Lord,
the maker of heaven and earth
bless you here.] **Amen.**

185 EXHORTATION
Ministers, musicians
from Psalm 135

Praise the Lord,
you servants of the Lord
who lead the worship of his house;
here in the house of our God,
praise the Lord,
sing praises to his name,
for he loves to hear you. **Amen.**

186 EXHORTATION
Church anniversary/dedication
from Psalm 150

Praise God in his sanctuary
and in his mighty heavens;
praise him for his acts of power
and for his surpassing greatness;
let everything that has breath
praise the Lord! **Amen.**

187 EXHORTATION
People of God, general
from Isaiah 12

Shout aloud, and sing for joy,
all his people:
for great is the Holy One, our Saviour. **Amen.**

188 EXHORTATION
Thanksgiving, rededication, general
from Jonah 2

Praise the Lord with a song of thanksgiving,
make good your promises to him:
salvation comes from the Lord! **Amen.**

189 EXHORTATION
General
from Romans 16

Let us give glory to God. **Amen.**

190 EXHORTATION
Trinity, God's majesty, general
from Revelation 19

Salvation and glory and power
belong to our God:
praise God! **Amen.**

191 EXHORTATION
Ascension, Trinity, God's majesty
from Revelation 19

The Lord, our mighty God, is king:
rejoice and be glad;
praise his greatness. **Amen.**

192 EXHORTATION
Ascension, Trinity, God's majesty
from Revelation 19 (alternative)

The Lord, our mighty God, is king:
let us rejoice and be glad;
let us praise his greatness. **Amen.**

193 EXHORTATION
Ascension, Trinity, general
from Revelation 19 (variant)

Praise God!
The Lord our almighty God is king!

Let us rejoice and be glad:
let us praise his greatness! Amen.

194 EXHORTATION
Thanksgiving, general
from Revelation 19

Let us rejoice and be glad
and give God the glory. **Amen.**

INTRODUCTION/
CONCLUSION
(READINGS)

195 BEFORE READING
God's word to us, general
from Deuteronomy 8, Matthew 4, Luke 4

We cannot survive on bread alone,
but we need every word
   that comes from God. **Amen.**

196 BEFORE READING
Advent, Epiphany, general
from 2 Samuel 22

You are our lamp, O Lord:
you turn our darkness into light. Amen.

197 BEFORE READING
Lent, general
from Jeremiah 9

Let us listen to the Lord;
let us hear to his word. **Amen.**

198 AFTER READING
from Mark 4

Those who have a mind to hear,
let them hear! **Amen.**

199 AFTER READING
Church anniversary/dedication, general
from Revelation 1–7

If you have a mind to hear,
listen to what the Spirit is saying
  to the church! **Amen.**

200 *RESPONSE AFTER READING*
Church anniversary/dedication, general
from Revelation 1–7 (alternative)

Hear what the Spirit is saying to the church:
Thanks be to God. Amen.

DECLARATION
OF FAITH
CREED

201 CREED
God: loving, faithful, satisfying
from Psalm 145

We believe in God,
who is gracious and compassionate,
slow to anger and rich in love.

We believe in God,
whose kingdom is everlasting,
whose dominion endures for ever.

We believe in God,
who is faithful to all his promises
and loving towards all he has made.

We believe in God,
who opens his hand
and satisfies the needs
of everything living. Amen.

202 CREED
Redemption, faith, forgiveness
from Isaiah 43

We believe in the Lord God, the Holy One,
Father, Son and Holy Spirit;
we are his witnesses and his servants.
He alone is the Lord,
apart from him there is no saviour;
he has revealed and saved and proclaimed;
he is our creator, our redeemer
    and our king;
it is he who blots out our transgressions
and remembers our sins no more. Amen.

203 CREED
Creation, people of God, Pentecost, renewal
from Isaiah 44

We believe in one God who made all things:
he alone stretched out the heavens
and spread out the earth;
he formed us in the womb,
he is our king and our redeemer –
the Lord almighty.

We belong to the lord –
we are his people
    and are called by his name;
he pours out his Spirit upon us
as water on a thirsty land:
we believe in one God, the almighty,
Father, Son and Holy Spirit. Amen.

204 CREED
Christmas, Incarnation, person of Christ
from John 1

Let us declare our faith in the Son of God:

In the beginning was the Word,
and the Word was with God,
and the Word was God.
Through him all things were made;
without him nothing was made
    that has been made.
In him was life,
and that life was the light of all people.

The Word became flesh
and lived for a while among us;
we have seen his glory,
the glory of the only Son of the Father,
full of grace and truth. Amen.

205 CREED
Lent, discipleship
from John 6, 11, 14 and 20

We believe and know
that Jesus is the Holy One of God.

We believe that he is the Christ,
the Son of God,
who was to come into the world.

We believe that he is in the Father
and the Father is in him.

We believe that Jesus is the Christ,
the Son of God,
and that by believing
we have life in his name. Amen.

206 CREED
Advent, Christmas, God's word,
  resurrection, faith, mission
from Romans 1

We believe in the Gospel,
promised by God long ago
  through the prophets,
written in the Holy Scriptures.

We believe in God's Son,
  our Lord Jesus Christ:
as to his humanity,
born a descendant of David;
as to his divinity,
shown with great power
  to be the Son of God
by his raising from death. Amen.

207 CREED
Easter, faith, witness, mission
from Romans 10

Jesus is Lord;
God has raised him from the dead.
By our faith we are put right with God,
and by our confession we are saved:
this we believe and this we proclaim. Amen.

208 CREED
Unity, Holy Communion, general
from 1 Corinthians 8 and 12

We believe in one God and Father;
from him all things come.

We believe in one Lord Jesus Christ;
through him we come to God.

We believe in one Holy Spirit;
in him we are baptized into one body.

We believe and trust in one God,
Father, Son and Holy Spirit. Amen.

209 CREED
Unity, Holy Communion, general
from 1 Corinthians 8 and 12 (responsive form)

There is one God and Father:
from him all things come.

There is one Lord Jesus Christ:
through him we come to God.

There is one Holy Spirit:
in him we are baptized into one body.

We believe and trust in one God:
Father, Son and Holy Spirit. Amen.

210 CREED
Renewal, gifts, ministries
from 1 Corinthians 12

We believe in the one Holy Spirit,
giver of different spiritual gifts.

We believe in one Jesus Christ,
Lord of various kinds of service.

We believe in one heavenly Father,
working in various ways.

We believe in one God,
Father, Son and Holy Spirit. Amen.

211 CREED

Easter, Scriptures
from 1 Corinthians 15

Christ died for our sins
in accordance with the Scriptures;
he was buried;
he was raised to life on the third day
in accordance with the Scriptures;
afterwards he appeared to his followers,
and to all the apostles:
this we have received and this we believe. Amen.

212 CREED

Ministry, Pentecost, general
from 2 Corinthians 1

It is Christ
to whom we belong.

It is the Father
who assures us of our salvation
and anoints us for his service.

It is the Spirit
by whom we are sealed in love for evermore.

We believe in one God,
Father, Son, and Holy Spirit. Amen.

213 CREED

Witness, ministry, renewal, heaven
from 2 Corinthians 4 and 5

We speak because we believe:

God, who raised the Lord Jesus Christ to life,
will also raise us up with Jesus
and take us together into his presence.
Though outwardly we are wasting away,
inwardly we are being renewed day by day;
we live by faith, and not by sight. Amen.

214 CREED

Passiontide, dedication, service, baptism
from Galatians 2

We have been crucified with Christ;
it is no longer we who live;
but Christ who lives in us.
The life we live in the body
we live by faith in the Son of God,
who loved us and gave himself for us. Amen.

215 CREED

Ascension, Church, national
from Ephesians 1

We believe
God raised from the dead
our Lord Jesus Christ
by his mighty power,
and seated him at his right hand in heaven,
far above all rule and authority,
power and dominion,
and every title that can be given,
not only in the present age
but also in the age to come.

God placed all things under his feet
and appointed him to be head over everything
for the church, which is his body,
the fullness of him who fills everything
everywhere and always. Amen.

216 CREED

People of God, family, general
from Ephesians 3

We believe in God the Father,
from whom every family
in heaven and on earth is named.

We believe in God the Son,
who lives in our hearts through faith,
and fills us with his love.

We believe in God the Holy Spirit,
who strengthens us with power from on high.

We believe in one God,
Father, Son, and Holy Spirit. Amen.

217 CREED
Unity, baptism
from Ephesians 4

We believe in one body, the church,
one Holy Spirit,
one hope to which we are called,
one Lord Jesus,
one faith,
one baptism,
one God and Father of all,
who is over all and through all
   and in all. Amen.

218 CREED
Ascension, Palm Sunday, person of Christ
from Philippians 2

Jesus Christ, the Son of God,
though he was divine,
did not cling to equality with God,
but made himself nothing.
Taking the form of a slave,
he became as we are;
as a man he humbled himself,
and was obedient to death –
even the death of the cross.

Therefore God has raised him on high,
and given him the name above every name:
that at the name of Jesus
every knee should bow,
and every voice proclaim
that Jesus Christ is Lord,
to the glory of God the Father. Amen.

219 CREED

Good Friday, reconciliation, person of
*   Christ, church*
from Colossians 1

We believe in Christ,
the image of God the invisible,
first-born of all creation;
in whom were created
all things in heaven and earth
seen and unseen –
states, powers, rulers and authorities;
all things were created through him and for him.

Christ is before all things,
in him all things hold together;
Christ is the head of the body, the church;
he is the beginning
and the first-born from the dead.

Christ over all things is supreme;
it is God's pleasure,
for all his fullness to live in him,
and by him to reconcile all things to himself,
making peace through the blood of the cross. Amen.

220 CREED
Christmas, church, national
from Colossians 1 (shorter version)

We believe in Christ,
the image of God the invisible,
first-born of all creation;
in whom were created
all things in heaven and earth
seen and unseen,
states, powers, rulers and authorities;
all things were created through him and for him.
He is before all things,
in him all things hold together.
He is the head of the body, the church;
he is the beginning
and the first-born from the dead. Amen.

221 CREED
Encouragement, strengthening, maturity,
*   spiritual protection*
from 2 Thessalonians 2 and 3

We believe in God the Father,
who loved us
and by his grace gave us
eternal encouragement and good hope.

We believe in God the Son,
who strengthens us,
and protects us from the evil one.

We believe in God the Holy Spirit,
who leads us to God the Father's love
and to the endurance
which is the gift of Christ.

We believe in one God,
Father, Son and Holy Spirit. Amen.

222 CREED
Mission, Ascension, general
from 1 Timothy 3

Let us proclaim the mystery of our faith:

We believe in one Lord Jesus Christ;
revealed in the flesh,
attested by the Spirit,
seen by the apostles,
proclaimed to the nations,
believed in throughout the world,
and taken up to glory. Amen.

223 CREED
Lent, people of God, heaven, general
from Titus 2 and 3

We believe in God the Father,
who has revealed his loving kindness to us,
and in his mercy saved us –
not for any good deed of our own,
but because he is merciful.

We believe in Jesus Christ,
who gave himself up for us
to free us from our sin,
and set us apart for himself –
a people eager to do good.

We believe in the Holy Spirit,
whom God poured out on us generously
through Christ our saviour –
so that justified by grace
we might become heirs
with the hope of eternal life. Amen.

224 CREED

Baptism, Pentecost, renewal, heaven
from Titus 3

We believe in God who saved us
not because of good things we have done,
but because of his mercy.
God saved us by the washing of rebirth,
and renewal by the Holy Spirit,
whom he poured out on us generously
through Jesus Christ our saviour;
so that justified by his grace
we might become heirs
with the hope of eternal life.
This is a trustworthy saying. Amen.

225 CREED

Christmas, creation, person of Christ
from Hebrews 1

We believe in God
who has spoken to us by his Son, Jesus Christ,
whom he appointed heir of all things,
through whom he made the worlds.
Christ is the radiance of God's glory,
the image of his being,
who upholds all things by his powerful word. Amen.

226 CREED

Temptation, prayer, Christ's intercession
from Hebrews 4

Let us hold firmly to the faith we profess:

We have a high priest
able to understand our weaknesses,
who has gone into heaven –
Jesus, the Son of God.
He was tempted in every way,
just as we are,
yet without sin.

Therefore we approach
the throne of grace
with confidence;
to receive mercy
and find grace to help us
in our time of need. Amen.

227 CREED

Atonement, general
from 1 Peter 3

We believe
Christ died for sins
once for all,
the just for the unjust,
to bring us to God;
he was put to death in the body,
but made alive by the Spirit;
he has gone up on high,
and is at God's right hand,
ruling over angels
and the powers of heaven. Amen.

228 CREED
RESPONSE
Before a Christological creed
from 1 John 5

Who can defeat the world?
Only the one who believes
that Jesus is the Son of God.

229 CREED
Study, wisdom, eternal life
from 1 John 5

We believe in Jesus Christ,
the Son of God,
and we have this truth in our hearts:
God has given us eternal life,
and this life is in his Son.
Whoever has the Son has life;
whoever does not have the Son of God
does not have life.

We believe
that the Son of God has come,
and has given us wisdom
to know the true God. Amen.

230 CREED
Church, Advent, Passiontide, All Saints,
   resurrection
from Revelation 1

We believe in God almighty,
the Lord, the first and the last,
who is, who was and who is to come.

We believe in Jesus Christ,
the faithful witness,
the first to be raised from death,
the ruler of the kings of the earth:
who loves us,
and by his sacrificial death
has freed us from our sins
and made us a kingdom of priests
to serve our God and Father. Amen.

231 CREED
Heaven, authority of Christ, resurrection
from Revelation 1

We believe in Jesus Christ,
before whom we fall down and worship
but need not be afraid:
he is the first and the last,
the living one;
he has authority over death
and the world of the dead,
for he was dead,
but now is alive for ever and ever. Amen.

232 CREED
Advent, Passiontide, worldwide church
from Revelation 4, 5 and 22

We believe in God the Father,
who created all things;
by his will they were created
and have their being.

We believe in God the Son, who was slain;
with his blood
he purchased us for God,
from every tribe and language
and people and nation.

We believe in God the Holy Spirit;
the Spirit and the Bride say, 'Come!'
Even so, come, Lord Jesus! Amen.

DEDICATION/
COMMENDATION/
DECLARATION

233 DEDICATION: PRESENTATION OF A BIBLE

Thanksgiving for a child, dedication, baptism
from Deuteronomy 6

Minister:
N and M (parents),
the words of this book
    that I give you today
are to be upon your hearts:
impress them on your children;
talk about them when you sit at home
and when you walk along the road,
when you lie down
and when you get up:
and may the Lord bless_____(child),
with the knowledge of his love. **Amen.**

234 DEDICATION: A CHILD

Dedication, baptism
from 1 Samuel 1

Parents:
Almighty God,
we bring our child, N, before you.
We prayed to you for *him*,
and you granted what we asked of you:
so now we give *him* to you.
For *his* whole life
    he shall be given over to you.
O God, we worship and adore you;
through Jesus, our Lord. **Amen.**

235 DEDICATION: HUSBAND AND WIFE
Marriage, marriage rededication
from Ephesians 5

Man:
I will love you
because Christ loves you;
as Christ gave himself up for me,
I will deny myself for you.

Woman:
As we yield to one another
out of reverence for Christ,
so in everything
I will yield to you.

Man:
Because Christ died for you,
I will love you, protect you, and pray for you,
that you may be holy and radiant in him
as together we obey his word.

Woman:
As together we reverence Christ
so I will give you my honour and respect.

Man:
In loving you I love myself:
As Christ feeds and cares for his own,
so I will feed and care for you.

Woman:
Even as we are both members of Christ's body,
so in a deep and secret sense
I will become part of you.

Man:
For you I leave my father and my mother;
and although we are two, we shall become one.

236 COMMENDATION: A WOMAN MINISTER
Installation, licensing
from Romans 16

Minister:
I commend to you
    our sister_____,
who serves/*to serve* the church at_____:
receive her in the Lord's name,
for she has been/*will be* a good friend to many people,
and is also a friend of mine.

237 COMMENDATION: A MAN MINISTER
Installation, licensing
from Philippians 2

Minister:
I commend to you_____,
to work and contend for the Lord
alongside us/*you*
God has blessed him,
and I eagerly commend him to you.
Receive him with joy
as a brother in the Lord;
show him respect,
because he gives his life
for the sake of the work of Christ,
in order to do
what you cannot do without him.

238 DECLARATION:
Baptism, renewal of Baptism vows
from Romans 6

Minister:
Do you know into what
all of us were baptized?

People:
In baptism
we were buried with Christ into death,
so that,
as Christ was gloriously raised from the dead
by the Father,
so we too may live a new life.

If we have been united with him in his death
we will be united with him in his resurrection.

Minister:
What, then,
shall we go on sinning so that grace may increase?

People:
No – we died to sin,
we may not live in it any longer;
our old self was crucified with Christ
    that our sinfulness might be done away;
so we should no longer be slaves to sin:
we must count ourselves dead to sin,
but alive to God
in Jesus Christ our Lord. **Amen.**

239 RESPONSE DECLARATION:
Before Holy Communion (see also thanksgiving, 356)
from Exodus 13, Matthew 26, Mark 14, Luke 22 and
  I Corinthians 11

Children/Minister:
What does this ceremony mean?

Adults:
When the time came
for Jesus to eat the Passover meal
   with his disciples,
on the night that he was betrayed
he took his place at the table.

While he was eating,
he took a piece of bread,
gave thanks to God and broke it.
Then he gave it to them saying,
'This is my body, which is for you.
Do this in remembrance of me.'

In the same way, after the supper
he took the cup, gave thanks to God,
and offered it to them saying,
'This cup is God's new covenant in my blood,
which is poured out for many
for the forgiveness of sins:
do this, whenever you drink it,
in remembrance of me.'
And they all drank from it.

Then Jesus said,
'I tell you the truth,
I will not drink wine again
until I drink the new wine
of the kingdom of God.'

This means that every time we eat this bread
and drink from this cup
we proclaim the Lord's death until he comes. **Amen.**

FOR OTHERS

240 FOR OTHERS: TYRANNY AND TERRORISM
from Psalm 10

Lord, you listen to the prayers of the lowly
and give them courage;
you hear the cries of the poor and the weak,
and you judge in their favour;
you take notice of trouble and suffering,
and are always ready to help:
look upon those who are oppressed –
where the proud persecute the poor,
where terrorists prey on the helpless,
where spies wait to trap the unwary and drag them away,
where the wicked crush their victims
and brute strength defeats the innocent,
where evil people do not fear you,
and say 'God does not care what we do'.
Lord God, break their power,
until evil has no part in your world
and you rule for ever and ever. **Amen.**

241 FOR OTHERS: IN WEAKNESS
from Psalm 25

Lord Jesus,
the friend of all who obey you;
who died that we might be forgiven,
to whom we look for help at all times,
who rescues us from danger:
be merciful to those who are lonely
    and to those who are weak;
relieve them of their worries
and save them out of their troubles;
consider their distress and suffering
and forgive them their sins;
help them to trust in you
and show them your salvation;
for your tender mercy's sake. **Amen.**

242 FOR OTHERS: IN TROUBLE
from Psalm 31

Be merciful, Lord,
to all those in trouble:
those who are exhausted,
those who are deep in sorrow,
those whose life is ebbing away,
those who are without friends,
those who are forgotten by the world;
Lord, we entrust them to your care.
In Jesus' name. **Amen.**

243 FOR OTHERS: OUR CHILDREN
from Psalm 78

Lord, let us not keep from our children
the things you have taught us,
and all we have received –
your wisdom, your power,
 and your great deeds:
for you told our ancestors to teach us,
that we in turn might instruct our children.
Help our children to be obedient to you –
to trust you
and remain faithful to you –
for ever. **Amen.**

244 FOR OTHERS: POLITICS
from Psalm 82

Come, Lord God, and rule the world:
all the nations are yours.
Let laws be just,
let justice be impartial,
let the rights of the poor and of children
 be defended,
help us to rescue the innocent
 from the power of evil men;
let the ignorant be taught,
let corruption be purged,
let righteousness prevail.
Come, Lord God, and rule the world:
all the nations are yours. **Amen.**

245 FOR OTHERS: FOR OUR LAND
from Psalm 85

Lord God,
you have been merciful to our land,
you have made us prosperous in the past,
you have forgiven us our sins
and pardoned our wrongdoing:
bring us back to faith, O God our saviour –
make us strong again;
show us your constant love
and give us your saving grace,
help us to listen to what you are saying
and to leave our foolish ways,
so that we might receive your peace.

Lord, help us to honour you,
so that your healthful presence may remain in our land:
then your love and our loyalty will meet,
our justice and your peace embrace;
our faith reach up from the earth,
and your goodness look down from heaven;
you will bless us,
and our righteousness will prepare your way;
through Jesus Christ our Lord. **Amen.**

246 FOR OTHERS: THE ELDERLY
from Psalm 90

Lord, you have always been our refuge:
before you created the hills,
before you brought the world into being,
you are God from all time –
and you will be God for ever;
a thousand years in your sight
are like yesterday, already gone.
We are like flowers
that spring up in the morning,
bloom in the afternoon
and die in the evening –
you know our weakness
and our sinfulness.
Lord, teach us how short our life is,
so that we may become wiser.

We pray for those whose days are numbered,
for those whose strength is fading;
we remember those
   whose later years are passing by,
those who are weak
or in trouble or sorrow:
Lord, have pity on them,
fill them each morning with your love
that they may praise you and be glad;
give them as much happiness
as they have had sadness;
let them see your strength
and your blessing upon their children.
O Lord, bless them and prosper them;
in the name of Jesus our redeemer. **Amen.**

247 FOR OTHERS: SEAFARERS
from Psalm 107

Lord of all goodness
and eternal love:
we pray for those who go to sea
and so earn their living;
we thank you that there they perceive
    your wonder and your majesty
and experience your awesome power –
waves stirred up and mighty winds blowing,
ships lifted high in the air
and plunged down into the depths.
In such danger
give them courage, reinforce their skill,
turn their prayers towards you
and save them from their distress;
calm the raging of the storm
and bring them home to the safety of their harbour;
then, Lord,
let them give thanks to you
for the wonderful things you have done for them
and so testify to your greatness;
for your glory's sake. **Amen.**

248 FOR OTHERS: MISSION
from Isaiah 61

Sovereign Lord,
you have anointed us with your Spirit
and have sent us to preach good news to the poor,
to bind up the broken-hearted,
to announce freedom to the captives
and release for the prisoners of darkness;
to proclaim your grace and your judgement,
to provide for those who mourn.
Bless all to whom we go;
bring your beauty into their lives –
joy instead of mourning
praise instead of despair;
through us, make them like trees you have planted
    rooted in righteousness,
that they may display your splendour;
through Jesus Christ our saviour. **Amen.**

249 FOR OTHERS: BLESSING
from Matthew 5

Bless, Lord, as you promised,
those who know they are spiritually poor,
that they may receive the kingdom of heaven;
bless those who mourn,
that they may be comforted;
bless the humble,
that they may inherit the earth;
bless those who hunger and thirst
   for your righteousness,
that they may be fully satisfied;
bless those who are pure in heart,
that they may see your face;
bless those who work for peace,
and make them your children;
bless those who are persecuted
   for doing what is right in your sight,
and bring them to your kingdom in heaven;
bless us all when we are insulted or persecuted,
or falsely accused because we are yours;
help us to rejoice and be glad
because you are keeping our great reward
for when we are with you in heaven for ever. **Amen.**

250 FOR OTHERS: THE DYING
from Luke 2

Lord,
now let your servant depart in peace,
for *his* eyes have seen your salvation;
through Jesus Christ,
the light of the world
and the glory of all your people. **Amen.**

251 FOR OTHERS: PREACHERS AND HEALERS
from Acts 4

Sovereign Lord,
you made the heaven, the earth and the sea,
and everything in them;
you spoke by the Holy Spirit
through the mouth of your servants of old:
enable your servants today
to speak your word with great boldness;
stretch out your hand to heal
and perform miraculous signs and wonders
through the name of your holy servant Jesus. **Amen.**

252 FOR OTHERS: FELLOWSHIP AND UNITY
from Romans 1

God our Father,
always, when we pray,
we thank you for our fellowship
    with others whom you love,
and have called to be your own people:
help us to share our spiritual blessings with them,
that we may be made strong together –
our faith helping them,
and their faith helping us;
through Jesus Christ our Lord. **Amen.**

253 FOR OTHERS: MARRIAGE
from Ephesians 5

The Woman:
Thank you, God my Father,
for N/*my bridegroom/my husband*:
as we all must submit to each other
   out of reverence for Christ
so help me to submit to him;
help me to be for him
beautiful in spirit,
pure, cleansed and radiant
through hearing your word;
and in the secret mystery of our union
help me to honour and respect him;
for Jesus' sake. **Amen.**

254 FOR OTHERS: MARRIAGE
from Ephesians 5

The Man:
Thank you, God my Father,
for N/*my bride/ my wife*:
help me to love her
because you love her,
to deny myself for her
just as you gave yourself up for me:
Help me to cherish her as my own body,
to provide for her and care for her
as you take care of us;
[help me for her sake
to leave my father and mother,
that we two may become one;]
through Jesus Christ our Lord. **Amen.**

255 FOR OTHERS: MISSION
from Colossians 4

God our Master in heaven, make us fair and just
in our dealings with others;
keep us persistent in prayer for them,
alert to their needs,
and constantly thankful;
open doors for us to proclaim the message
    about the secret of Christ;
help us to speak as we should, to make it clear.
Keep us wise in the way we act
    towards those who do not believe,
help us always to make good use
    of every opportunity we have;
let our conversation be attractive
    and interesting to them,
and teach us how to give the right answer to everyone,
through Jesus Christ our Lord. **Amen.**

FOR OURSELVES

256 FOR OURSELVES: BEFORE MEDITATION
from 1 Samuel 3

Speak, Lord,
for your servant
is listening. **Amen.**

257 FOR OURSELVES: BEFORE PREACHING
from 1 Samuel 3 (alternative)

Speak, Lord,
for your servants
are listening. **Amen.**

258 FOR OURSELVES: IN TIME OF TROUBLE
from 2 Chronicles 20

Lord God of heaven,
you rule over states and nations;
power and might are in your hand,
and no one can withstand you.
We bow in your presence
and cry out to you
   in the name of Jesus;
we have no power to face the enemy that attacks us,
we do not know what to do –
but our eyes are on you. **Amen.**

259 FOR OURSELVES: WISDOM
from Job 38

Lord,
you laid the earth's foundations;
   you placed its cornerstone;
while the morning stars sang together
and all the angels shouted for joy
you set limits for the sea and said,
   'This far and no further!'
You gave orders to the morning
and showed the dawn its place;
you moulded the earth until it took shape.
You alone know the springs of the sea;
you alone comprehend the vastness of the universe;
you alone know the laws of heaven.
Lord, give wisdom to our hearts
and understanding to our minds. **Amen.**

260 FOR OURSELVES: FRUITFULNESS
from Psalm 1

God, our guide and protector,
you condemn the wicked,
and blow them away
  like straws in the wind:
help us to reject the ways of evil people
and not to follow the example of sinners,
but instead to find joy
  in obeying your law
and in studying it day and night.
Let us be like trees
growing beside the water,
whose leaves do not dry up,
so that our lives may bear the fruit
  of your Spirit;
in Jesus Christ our Lord. **Amen.**

261 FOR OURSELVES: FOR PROTECTION
For protection
from Psalm 3

Lord, our shield from danger:
when we call to you for help,
hear our prayer from heaven;
when people turn against us
and mock our faith,
restore our courage
and bring us victory;
when troubles surround us on all sides,
give us rest, help us sleep,
and protect us all night long.
Lord come to us,
Lord save us;
bless us your people,
for we overcome in you alone. **Amen.**

262 FOR OURSELVES: WHEN OTHERS PROSPER
from Psalm 4

God our defender and protector,
you help us in our trouble
and guard us awake and sleeping;
you have called us to be righteous
and you possess us in your love:
be merciful now
and hear our prayer.
Let us not be hurt
when people insult us;
save us from following others in worthless pursuits;
help us to fear you and not to sin,
to offer you our lives as a sacrifice
and to put our trust in you:
for the joy you give
   is greater than their prosperity,
and perfect peace comes from you alone;
through Jesus Christ our Lord. **Amen.**

263 FOR OURSELVES: IN SORROW OR WEARINESS
from Psalm 6

Lord,
you alone hear my weeping
and listen to my cry for help:
don't be angry with me,
don't punish me.
I am worn out – have pity on me,
I am completely exhausted –
   give me back my strength,
I am deeply humbled – come and save me.

Lord, what is the point of it all?
How long will it be
   before my prayer is answered?

Lord, it is in the night that I am so unhappy –
sometimes my eyes hurt
and my pillow is wet with tears:
come to my rescue,
and drive the enemy away;
through Jesus my redeemer. **Amen.**

264 FOR OURSELVES: SINCERITY
from Psalm 15

Lord God,
make us fit to enter your presence;
help us to worship you sincerely
and to obey you in everything.
Lead us always to do what is right:
let our words be true and sincere;
keep us from slandering others –
neither hurting our friends
nor failing our neighbours.
Teach us not to follow those whom you reject,
but to honour all who obey you.
Strengthen us always to keep our promise
no matter what it costs;
to lend without expecting anything in return,
never to accept bribes,
and to uphold the rights of the innocent:
so may we be secure in your love;
through Jesus Christ our saviour. **Amen.**

265 FOR OURSELVES: GUIDANCE
from Psalm 16

God our protector –
we trust in you for safety,
we depend on you for all we need,
all good things come from you:
we commit our future into your hands –
guide us by day and teach us by night,
be near us so that nothing can shake us,
make us always aware of your presence,
show us the path that leads to life,
let your Spirit fill us with joy
and let your service
   be our delight for ever. **Amen.**

266 FOR OURSELVES: OBEDIENCE
from Psalm 17

Lord God,
you listen to our prayers,
and you do what is right:
search our hearts
and cleanse them from every evil desire,
purge our tongues that we speak no evil –
   even if others do;
teach us to obey your commands
and not to follow the path of violence,
to walk in your way
and never to stray from it.
Turn to us, hear us,
and reveal to us your wonderful love
in Jesus Christ our Lord. **Amen.**

267 FOR OURSELVES: CLEANSING
from Psalm 19

Lord God, our refuge and our redeemer,
may our words and our thoughts
    be acceptable to you.
We cannot see our own failings:
save us, O Lord, from our hidden faults
and keep us from wilful sins –
don't let them get a hold over us.
Make us perfect in Christ Jesus,
and for his sake deliver us from evil.
May our words and our thoughts
always be acceptable to you,
Lord God, our refuge and our redeemer. **Amen.**

268 FOR OURSELVES: BEFORE WORSHIP
from Psalm 19

May the words of my mouth
and the meditation of my heart
be pleasing in your sight,
O Lord, my Rock and my Redeemer. **Amen.**

269 FOR OURSELVES: BEFORE PREACHING
from Psalm 19 (alternative)

May the words of my mouth
and the thoughts of all our hearts
be pleasing in your sight,
O Lord, our Rock and our Redeemer. **Amen.**

270 FOR OURSELVES: GOD'S PRESENCE
from Psalm 23

Lord,
you are my shepherd;
you give me all I need,
you make me lie down in green pastures,
you lead me beside still waters,
you restore my soul,
you guide me in the paths of righteousness.
Even though I walk through the valley
    of the shadow of death
you are with me, and you comfort me.
Let your goodness and love
    follow me all the days of my life,
and let me live in your presence for ever. **Amen.**

271 FOR OURSELVES: GOD'S PRESENCE
from Psalm 23 (alternative)

Lord, be
you are our shepherd;
you give us all we need,
you make us lie down in green pastures,
you lead us beside still waters,
you restore our soul,
you guide us in paths of righteousness.
Even though we walk through the valley
    of the shadow of death
you are with us, and you comfort us.
Let your goodness and your love
    follow us all the days of our life,
until we live in your presence for ever. **Amen.**

272 FOR OURSELVES: FORGIVENESS
from Psalm 25

O Lord,
I pray to you because I trust you,
and because you have always shown me
   kindness and constant love:
as you have promised –
forgive me the errors of my ways,
my sins when I was younger,
and my many sins since then;
teach me to live by your truth,
and show me the path to follow;
through Jesus Christ my saviour. **Amen.**

273 FOR OURSELVES: GOODNESS
from Psalm 25

Lord God, our saviour,
we trust in you:
show us your way,
teach us your paths,
guide us in your truth,
forgive our sins,
fix our eyes on you,
release us from the snares of evil;
strengthen us when we are weak,
come to us when we are lonely,
free our hearts from sorrow,
guard our lives in danger,
keep us in truth and honesty;
let our hope be always in you
our Lord God and our saviour. **Amen.**

274 FOR OURSELVES: IN TROUBLE
from Psalm 31

Be merciful, Lord,
for I am in trouble;
my eyes are sore with crying,
I am exhausted,
I am deep in sorrow,
my life is ebbing away,
my neighbours seem to ignore me,
my friends appear to have forgotten me:
Lord, I trust in you,
I place myself in your care. **Amen.**

275 FOR OURSELVES: DELIVERANCE
from Psalm 31

O Lord, we trust in you,
we say, 'You are our God';
our times are in your hands.
Deliver us from all that would harm us
and from any who would hurt us;
let your face shine upon us,
and save us in your unfailing love;
through Jesus Christ our Lord. **Amen.**

276 FOR OURSELVES: A PRAYER OF TRUST
from Psalm 33

O Lord,
we wait for you in hope;
you are our help and our shield;
in you our hearts rejoice,
for we trust your holy name.
Let your unfailing love
   rest upon us, Lord,
for we put our hope in you. **Amen.**

277 FOR OURSELVES: EMPTINESS
from Psalms 42 and 43

As a deer thirsts for streams of water
so I yearn for you, my God;
for I long to worship in your presence.
I remember days past
when I went with others to praise you,
but now I am heartbroken,
and so very far away:
send your light and your truth
to lead me back to worship in your house,
once again to sing your praises,
my saviour and my God. **Amen.**

278 FOR OURSELVES: RENEWAL OF HEART AND MIND
from Psalm 51

Lord, you require in us
sincerity and truth:
fill our minds with your wisdom,
make us content in your service;
create in us a new heart
and put a loyal spirit in us.
Do not banish us from your presence,
or take your Holy Spirit from us;
give us the joy that comes from your salvation,
and make us willing to obey you;
through Jesus Christ our Lord. **Amen.**

279 FOR OURSELVES: IN TROUBLE
from Psalm 55

Lord, when we pray,
don't turn away from us:
when we are worn out with our worries
and crushed by our troubles,
then hear us and answer our cry;
for some of us are threatened by the enemy,
others opposed by evil people;
there are those who are terrified of dying,
and some who live in fear of violence;
others have friends who give them pain.
Our God, you have ruled from eternity:
teach us to leave our troubles with you,
so that you may defend us;
through Jesus Christ our saviour. **Amen.**

280 FOR OURSELVES: IN DISTRESS
from Psalm 77

When we cry aloud to you, our God,
hear us and answer our prayer.
When we are in trouble,
when we are anxious and feel discouraged,
when in the night we cannot find comfort,
when we lie awake and think about you,
when we are so worried that we cannot speak,
when our faith falters
   and we feel you have rejected us:
then, Lord, remind us of your great deeds;
speak to us about your strong salvation.
When we cry aloud to you, our God,
hear us and answer our prayer. **Amen.**

281 FOR OURSELVES: HOME AND WORK
from Psalm 112

Lord of our praise,
strengthen us,
that we may honour you
by obeying your commandments;
prosper our children,
and their children,
and bless our families.

Lord of our righteousness,
bring light out of darkness
in our places of work;
make us merciful, kind and just,
make us generous and honest,
let us be remembered for doing good.

Lord of our trust,
make our faith strong:
so that when bad news comes
we shall not be worried or afraid,
but able to leave the outcome to you.

Lord of our hope,
make us merciful to the needy,
with a kindness that never fails
but confounds the wicked and the careless;
help us to give as you gave to us
in Jesus Christ our Lord. **Amen.**

282 FOR OURSELVES: GOD'S LAWS
from Psalm 119 (1–8)

Lord, you have given us your laws
and told us to obey them faithfully:
help us to pay attention to them,
so that we shall not be put to shame;
and to learn them,
that we may praise you with a pure heart;
through Jesus Christ our Lord. **Amen.**

283 FOR OURSELVES: STRENGTH
from Psalm 119 (25–32)

Lord, I have failed,
and I need you to revive me
   as you have promised;
I have confessed all my sin,
and I know that you have heard me.

I am overcome with remorse:
in your goodness, make me stronger,
keep me from going the wrong way,
teach me your law,
help me to be obedient,
and give me more understanding;
through my saviour Jesus Christ. **Amen.**

284 FOR OURSELVES: STRENGTH
from Psalm 119 (25–32) (alternative)

Lord, we have failed,
and we need you to revive us
  as you have promised;
we have confessed all our sin,
and we know that you have heard us.
We are overcome with remorse:
in your goodness make us stronger,
keep us from going the wrong way,
teach us your law,
help us to be obedient,
and give us more understanding;
through our saviour Jesus Christ. **Amen.**

285 FOR OURSELVES: GOD'S WORD
from Psalm 119 (105–112)

O God,
let your word be
a lamp to guide me,
a light for my path,
my joy all the days of my life
and my possession for eternity;
through Jesus Christ our Lord. **Amen.**

286 FOR OURSELVES: GOD'S WORD
from Psalm 119 (105–112; alternative)

O God,
let your word be
a lamp to guide us,
a light for our path,
our joy all the days of our life
and our possession for eternity;
through Jesus Christ our Lord. **Amen.**

287 FOR OURSELVES: PROTECTION
from Psalm 119 (113–118)

Lord,
my defender and protector,
in your promise I put my trust:
strengthen me and let me live,
hold me and keep me safe;
through Jesus my redeemer. **Amen.**

288 FOR OURSELVES: PROTECTION
from Psalm 119 (113–118; alternative)

Lord,
our defender and protector,
in your promise we put our trust:
strengthen us and we shall live,
hold us and we will be safe;
through Jesus our redeemer. **Amen.**

289 FOR OURSELVES: MERCY
from Psalm 119 (129–136)

Lord,
you have mercy on those who love you:
turn to us and forgive us –
as you have promised;
keep us from falling,
preserve us from all evil,
bless us with your presence
and teach us your laws. **Amen.**

290 FOR OURSELVES: MERCY
from Psalm 119 (129–136; alternative)

Lord,
you have mercy on those who love you:
turn to me and forgive me –
as you have promised;
keep me from falling,
preserve me from all evil,
bless me with your presence
and teach me your laws. **Amen.**

291 FOR OURSELVES: NIGHT AND MORNING
from Psalm 119 (145–152)

Lord,
in the night
  when I lie awake
and think about what you have taught me:
hear me,
and because your love is faithful
show me your mercy,
and preserve my life.

Lord,
in the morning
when I call to you
and place my hope in your promise,
answer me again;
through Jesus my redeemer. **Amen.**

292 FOR OURSELVES: RESCUE
from Psalm 119 (169–176)

Lord, I wander like a lost sheep:
so come to look for me;
let my cry for help reach you,
listen to my prayer and save me,
give me life,
that I may praise and worship you
  for ever. **Amen.**

293 FOR OURSELVES: RESCUE
from Psalm 119 (169–176; alternative)

Lord, we wander like lost sheep:
come to look for us;
let our cries for help reach you,
listen to our prayers and save us,
give us life,
that we may praise and worship you
    for ever. **Amen.**

294 FOR OURSELVES: FAMILIES
from Psalm 127

Lord,
help us build our homes,
because if you are not with us
our toil is useless;
help us protect our families,
because if you do not guard them
we waste our efforts.
Help us in our work –
our over-working, too, is useless,
because you can bless us equally
    when we are asleep!

The children you have given us,
they are a real blessing –
our great happiness:
thank you, Lord. **Amen.**

295 FOR OURSELVES: HUMILITY
from Psalm 131

Lord God,
keep our hearts from pride,
keep our eyes from haughty looks,
keep our minds from arrogance,
keep our spirits calm –
in childlike dependence upon you:
for you are our hope now and always. **Amen.**

296 FOR OURSELVES: HUMILITY
from Psalm 131 (alternative)

Lord God,
keep my heart from pride,
keep my eyes from haughty looks,
keep my mind from arrogance,
keep my spirit calm –
in childlike dependence upon you:
for you are my hope now and always. **Amen.**

297 FOR OURSELVES: RIGHT BEHAVIOUR
from Psalm 141

Lord,
hear us when we call to you –
come quickly to save us;
let our prayers rise up before you
    like incense,
and the lifting of our hands
be as a sacrifice of praise.

Lord,
set a guard over what we say,
keep watch over the door of our lips;
don't let our hearts be drawn to what is evil,
    to do wicked things;
make us take notice of good people
that we may correct our ways by theirs.
Above all, keep our eyes fixed on you;
for you alone are able to protect us
    from the snares of death,
and to make us live in safety. **Amen.**

298 FOR OURSELVES: RIGHT BEHAVIOUR
from Psalm 141 (alternative)

Lord,
hear me when I call to you –
come quickly to save me;
let my prayer rise up before you
   like incense,
and the lifting of my hands
   be as a sacrifice of praise,

Lord,
set a guard over what I say,
keep watch over the door of my lips;
don't let my heart be drawn to what is evil,
   to do wicked things;
make me take notice of good people
that I may correct my ways by theirs.
Above all, keep my eyes fixed on you;
for you alone are able to protect me
   from the snares of death,
and to make me live in safety. **Amen.**

299 FOR OURSELVES: RIGHT BEHAVIOUR
from Psalm 141 (variant)

Lord, we call to you:
come quickly in answer to our prayer.
We lift our hearts and hands to you:
set a guard over our mouths,
a sentry at the door of our lips;
keep us from wanting to do wrong
or joining in evil deeds.
Help us to accept correction
given to us in kindness from good people,
prompt us to pray for the wicked,
but to reject their enticing ways;
for the glory of your name. **Amen.**

300 FOR OURSELVES: IN TEMPTATION
from Psalm 141

Sovereign Lord,
when the enemy seeks to tempt and ensnare us,
fix our eyes on you,
that we may pass by in safety:
then yours shall be the glory;
through Jesus our redeemer. **Amen.**

301 FOR OURSELVES: IN TEMPTATION
from Psalm 141 (alternative)

Sovereign Lord,
when the enemy seeks to tempt and ensnare me,
fix my eyes on you,
that I may pass by in safety:
then yours shall be the glory;
through Jesus my redeemer. **Amen.**

302 FOR OURSELVES: MERCY
from Psalm 143

O Lord,
hear our prayer as we cry for your mercy;
in your faithfulness and righteousness
come to help us.

Do not bring us to judgement,
for no one is innocent before you.
We remember days gone by,
and think about all you have done for us;
we lift our hands to you
and our souls thirst for you:
O Lord,
hear our prayer
as we cry to you for mercy.

Answer us now, Lord,
don't hide yourself from us;
remind us each morning of your constant love,
for we put our trust in you:
O Lord,
hear our prayer
as we cry to you for mercy.

We pray to you:
show us the way we should go,
rescue us from our enemies,
teach us to do your will;
by your good spirit
lead us in a safe path.
O Lord,
hear our prayer
as we cry to you for mercy. Amen.

303 FOR OURSELVES: TRUST
from Psalm 143

Lord God,
as we remember days gone by,
and think about all you have done for us,
our souls thirst for you
and we lift our hands to you in prayer.
Answer us now, Lord,
don't hide yourself from us;
remind us each morning of your constant love:
for we put our trust in you,
through Jesus Christ our Lord. **Amen.**

304 FOR OURSELVES: GUIDANCE
from Psalm 143 (variant)

Lord God,
let us hear your voice in the morning,
for in you shall be our trust;
show us the way that we should walk in,
for we lift up our souls to you;
teach us to do the thing that pleases you,
for you are our God.
Let your loving Spirit
   lead us in the right path,
for your name's sake. **Amen.**

305 FOR OURSELVES: GOD'S PRESENCE
from Isaiah 33

Lord,
be gracious to us,
for we long for you.
Be our strength every morning,
and our salvation in time of distress,
through Jesus our redeemer. **Amen.**

306 FOR OURSELVES: GOD'S PRESENCE
from Isaiah 33 (alternative)

Lord,
be gracious to me,
for I long for you;
be my strength every morning,
and my help in time of trouble.
Thank you, Lord. **Amen.**

307 FOR OURSELVES: GOD'S BLESSING
from Isaiah 35

Lord God,
lead us in the way of holiness,
cleanse us for our journey
and teach us to be wise;
guard your redeemed,
crown your ransomed ones
   with everlasting joy;
let sorrow and sighing flee away
and gladness overtake us;
in Jesus Christ our saviour. **Amen.**

308 FOR OURSELVES: IN WEARINESS
from Isaiah 40

Lord,
everlasting God,
creator of the ends of the earth,
you never grow tired or weary
and no one can fathom your wisdom:
when we feel weak
   increase in us your power,
when we are tired
   refresh us,
when we stumble and fall
   lift us up.
Lord, you are our hope:
renew us and strengthen us
   now and always. **Amen.**

309 FOR OURSELVES: OUR NATION
from Isaiah 66

Lord almighty,
heaven is your throne
and earth your footstool;
our country/*city*/*town*/*village* is in pain:
extend to us your peace like a river,
and restore to us prosperity.
As a mother comforts her children,
so comfort us –
that our hearts may rejoice,
and that we may flourish like a garden
tended by your hand;
Lord, in your mercy hear us. **Amen.**

310 FOR OURSELVES: HEALING
from Jeremiah 17

Lord,
heal us
and we shall be healed;
save us
and we shall be saved:
and the praise shall be yours alone. **Amen.**

311 FOR OURSELVES: HEALING
from Jeremiah 17 (alternative)

Lord,
heal me
and I will be healed;
save me
and I will be saved:
and the praise shall be yours alone. **Amen.**

312 FOR OURSELVES: RESPONSE TO GOD
from Matthew 13 (Mark 4 and Luke 8)

Lord God,
make us receptive to your voice:
open deaf ears,
soften hard hearts,
concentrate distracted minds,
deepen shallow emotions;
send your Spirit, Lord,
that your word may take root and grow in us,
so that we may flourish in your service
to the glory of your name. **Amen.**

313 FOR OURSELVES: ABOUT THE END OF TIME/
ADVENT
from Mark 13

When the skies grow dark and buildings fall,
then hear us, Lord:
have mercy on us.

When deceivers come
and the nations rise in anger,
then hear us, Lord:
have mercy on us.

When the famines begin,
and when the earth shakes
  to bring the future to birth,
then hear us, Lord:
have mercy on us.

When we stand for a witness,
when we are arrested and betrayed,
then hear us, Lord:
have mercy on us.

When the sun is darkened
and the moon fails to give us light,
and the stars fall from the sky,
then hear us, Lord:
have mercy on us.

When you come in your great power and glory
  with your angels from heaven,
have mercy, Lord:
gather us from the four winds,
from the ends of the earth,
to be with you for ever. Amen.

314 FOR OURSELVES: SALVATION IN CHRIST
from John 3

Holy Spirit of God,
invisible like the wind,
we do not see you moving among us,
but the effect we see:
come to our hearts
that we may be renewed and reborn.
Open our minds
that we may perceive your kingdom,
lift up our eyes
to where the cross of Christ stands
   for our healing;
that we might believe,
and in believing not die
but have eternal life;
through him
who in your love for us
you sent into the world,
Jesus Christ our Lord. **Amen.**

315 FOR OURSELVES: FAITH
from Romans 4

O God,
because of our faith
you have accepted us as righteous;
you bring the dead to life,
and by your command bring into being
things which did not exist:
help us to believe and to hope
when there is no earthly reason for hoping;
let our faith not leave us,
and let us not doubt your word.
But fill us with love, that we may give you praise,
sure that you are able to do what you promise;
through Jesus Christ our Lord. **Amen.**

316 FOR OURSELVES: DEDICATION/EASTER/BAPTISM
from Romans 14

Our Saviour Jesus Christ,
Lord of the living and the dead,
you died and rose again to life:
let us not live for ourselves alone,
nor die for ourselves alone;
that whether we live or die
we may belong to you for ever. **Amen.**

317 FOR OURSELVES: GOD'S MERCY
from 1 Corinthians 13

When we lose our patience,
when we are unkind,
when we are envious,
when we are rude or proud,
when we are selfish or irritable,
and when we will not forgive:
have mercy on us, O God.

Help us not to delight in evil,
but to rejoice in the truth;
help us always to protect, to trust,
to hope and to persevere:
so let us love one another –
until we see you face to face,
and know at last
just how much you love us. **Amen.**

318 FOR OURSELVES: RESURRECTION
from 1 Corinthians 15

God of the imperishable kingdom:
sound the trumpet,
wake us from our long sleep,
raise us in Christ,
clothe us with immortality,
swallow up death in victory!

O mighty God,
receive the thanks
    of your redeemed people,
to whom you give the victory
through our Lord Jesus Christ. **Amen.**

319 FOR OURSELVES: ABOUT OUR WEAKNESS
from 2 Corinthians 12

God our redeemer, .
you have taught us in your word
that your grace is sufficient for us
and that your power is made perfect in weakness:
help us to acknowledge our weaknesses
so that Christ's power may rest upon us;
to delight in hardships, persecutions
    and difficulties;
and to know when we are weak,
so that we may be strong
through Jesus Christ our Lord. **Amen.**

320 FOR OURSELVES: LOVE AND MATURITY
from Ephesians 3

God and Father
from whom the whole family
    in heaven and on earth is named:
bless us with the riches of your glory;
make us inwardly strong,
and powerful in your Spirit;
let Christ live in our hearts by faith;
that, rooted in love and founded on love,
we may surely grasp with all your people
how broad and long, how high and deep
is his love.
So may we know that love which passes knowledge,
and be filled with all your fulness;
through Jesus Christ our Lord. **Amen.**

321 FOR OURSELVES: CHRIST-LIKENESS
from Philippians 3

God of grace,
we have no righteousness of our own,
but you give us the righteousness
   which comes by faith in Christ:
give us also the mind which counts everything loss
   compared to his surpassing greatness.
May we gain him, and be found in him:
may we know him and the power of his resurrection;
may we rejoice
   to share the fellowship of his sufferings,
becoming like him in his death
to attain the resurrection from the dead
in Jesus our Lord. **Amen.**

322 FOR OURSELVES: PEACE
from Philippians 4

God of peace,
cause us to rejoice in you always,
make us gentle to everyone,
keep us from being anxious about anything –
help us to ask you for what we need,
   with thanksgiving;
and let your peace
guard our hearts and minds
in Jesus Christ our Lord. **Amen.**

323 FOR OURSELVES: HOPE
from 1 Thessalonians 4

Lord Jesus,
you will come from heaven with a loud command,
with the voice of the archangel,
and with the trumpet-call of God:
confirm our faith in your death and resurrection
so that we shall not grieve,
as others do who have no hope,
for those who have fallen asleep in Christ;
but believe that you will bring them with you
to meet us in the skies
that we may be with you for ever. **Amen.**

324 FOR OURSELVES: STRENGTH AND SERENITY
from 2 Thessalonians 2

God our Father,
you loved us
and by your grace gave us
eternal courage and good hope:
encourage our hearts,
and strengthen us
in every good deed and word;
let the Spirit of peace
give us peace at all times
and in every way;
and may the grace of the Lord Jesus Christ
be with us all. **Amen.**

325 FOR OURSELVES: CONFIDENCE IN CHRIST
from Hebrews 4

Jesus,
Son of God,
our high priest who has gone into the heavens,
you are able to understand our weaknesses
for you have been tempted in every way,
just as we are – yet without sin:
give us confidence,
that we may approach the throne of grace
to receive mercy,
and find grace to help us in our time of need;
to the glory of God the Father. **Amen.**

326 FOR OURSELVES: FOR MERCY AND HELP
from Hebrews 4

O God, our Father,
whose Son Jesus Christ
was tempted in every way as we are
but did not sin,
we approach your throne with confidence,
knowing that he understands:
in our weakness show us your mercy
and, because we need your grace,
help us for Jesus' sake. **Amen.**

327 FOR OURSELVES: BEFORE PRAYER
from Hebrews 4 (variant)

Lord, give us confidence
to approach your throne
and receive mercy and grace
to help us in our need. **Amen.**

328 FOR OURSELVES: ASSURANCE
from Hebrews 11

Living God,
give us faith to be sure of what we hope for,
and certain of what we do not see;
to believe that you are,
and that you reward those who truly seek you:
so may we please you
and receive what you have promised;
in Jesus Christ our Lord. **Amen.**

329 FOR OURSELVES: SUFFERING
from 1 Peter 1

God and Father of our Lord Jesus Christ,
shield us through our faith and by your power.
If we are called to suffering in any kind of trial
help us to rejoice,
and to know that it comes so that our faith,
more precious than perishable gold
   which is refined by fire,
may prove enduring
to the praise and glory and honour
of Jesus Christ our Lord. **Amen.**

330 FOR OURSELVES: THAT WE MAY WALK IN GOD'S LIGHT
from 1 John 1

O God, you are light,
and in you there is no darkness at all:
give us grace
no longer to walk in darkness,
but to walk in the light;
to live by the truth,
to have fellowship with you
   and with one another,
purified from all sin
by the blood of your Son,
Jesus Christ our Lord. **Amen.**

THANKSGIVING

331 THANKSGIVING
Church anniversary/dedication, giving
from 1 Chronicles 29

Lord God of our fathers,
may you be praised for ever and ever!
You are great and powerful, glorious,
   splendid and majestic;
everything in heaven and on earth is yours,
and you are king, supreme ruler over all;
all wealth and honour come from you,
you rule with strength and power:
now, our God,
we give you thanks,
and praise your glorious name. **Amen.**

PGIMF 2005 Ps 8

332 THANKSGIVING
Creation
from Psalm 8

O Lord our Lord,
we thank you that your name
   through all the earth is majesty,
that you have set your glory in the skies,
but yet receive praise from the lips of children.
We gaze at the work of your fingers,
the moon and the stars which you have set in place,
and we praise you that you even think of us;
you make us lower than the angels,
only to crown us with glory and honour.
O Lord our Lord,
we thank you in Jesus' name. **Amen.**

333 THANKSGIVING
International, times of trouble
from Psalm 9

O Lord God,
we thank you that you reign for ever,
that you have set your throne for judgement;
that you will rule the world in righteousness
and govern the nations with justice.
We praise you that you are a refuge for the oppressed
and a rock in time of trouble:
we who know your name will trust you,
for you have never forsaken those who love you.
O Lord God, we thank you. **Amen.**

334 THANKSGIVING
Dependence on God
from Psalm 16

God, my protector,
I trust you for my safety;
you are my Lord
and every good thing I have comes from you:
how wonderful is the fellowship
   of those who love you –
my greatest joy is to be with them!
You are my Lord alone,
and you give me all I need;
my future is in your hands.
By day you guide me, by night you teach me –
I am always conscious of your presence;
when you are near, nothing can shake me.
Thank you, God;
thank you in Jesus' name. **Amen.**

335 THANKSGIVING
Easter Communion
from Psalm 16 (variant)

O Lord, you are our Lord,
the only source of everything good;
we delight to be with those who love you.
You have given us this bread and this cup –
our hearts rejoice, our voices are triumphant;
we look forward with hope
because you did not let your Son perish
and have not abandoned us to death.
Through his mighty Resurrection
you have made known to us the way of life,
you have filled us with joy in your presence,
and given us the promise of glory
   at your right hand for evermore. **Amen.**

336 THANKSGIVING
Redemption, recovery
from Psalm 18

Lord, how I love you!
You are my defender, my protector,
my strong fortress;
with you I am safe.
I call to you, and you rescue me:
how I praise you, Lord! **Amen.**

I was near death,
and the waters
had almost closed above my head;
in my danger I called to you
and you heard me.
You reached down to me
and pulled me out of disaster.
How I praise you, Lord! **Amen.**

337 THANKSGIVING
Church anniversary/dedication
from Psalm 26

Lord God,
we thank you that in Christ
  we are declared righteous;
that we have your constant love to guide us,
and your faithfulness to lead us:
help us not to keep company with evil,
but to shun hypocrisy;
bring us to worship in your presence,
hear us as we sing hymns of thanksgiving,
strengthen us to proclaim
  the wonderful things you have done.

We love the place where we worship you, Lord –
where we sense your glory,
where in the fellowship of your people
  we praise you:
thank you, Lord. **Amen.**

338 THANKSGIVING
Trinity, All Saints, sea, church anniversary
from Psalm 29

O Lord God,
we acknowledge your strength and glory;
we worship you in the splendour of your holiness.
You thunder across the mighty waters,
your word is powerful,
your voice is majestic;
all in your temple cry 'Glory!'
Lord,
we thank you that you sit as king
  enthroned for ever;
we thank you that you give strength to your people
and speak to us your words of peace. **Amen.**

339 THANKSGIVING
Lent, for recovery
from Psalm 30

Lord God,
I want to praise you
because you have saved me;
I was on the way down
   to the depths of despair,
I cried to you for help
and you rescued me, and restored my life.

I praise you, and thank you
as I recall what you have done,
because the night of my tears
has given place to the morning of joy.

I was proud
   and thought I could do without you –
you were patient with me.
When you hid yourself from me
I was suddenly afraid;
then I felt I was dying,
   and I begged you for help;
but you have changed my sadness
   into a joyful dance,
you have taken away my sorrow
and surrounded me with joy.
So I will not keep silent,
   I will sing your praise:
you are my God,
and I will give thanks to you for ever! **Amen.**

340 THANKSGIVING
Lent, forgiveness
from Psalm 32

Lord,
thank you that you are willing to forgive our sins –
how happy we are when we have confessed them!
When you have forgiven us
we need pretend no longer;
while we do *not* confess them,
we are full of guilt and remorse
    day and night,
and our strength drains away;
but when we confess our sins to you,
and do not try to conceal them,
then you forgive us in Jesus;
when we have his righteousness
then we can rejoice and be glad,
then to obey you is to be happy.
Thank you, Lord. **Amen.**

341 THANKSGIVING
Providence, answers to prayer
from Psalm 34

Lord, we thank you again
and praise you for what you have done;
we proclaim your greatness,
we exalt your name together:
for you answer all our prayers
and free us from our fears,
you are near to those who are discouraged,
you save those who have lost all hope.
Lord, you are good to us,
and we are happy in your care:
so we would honour and obey you
and thank you with all our heart. **Amen.**

342 THANKSGIVING
Holy Communion
from Psalm 36

We thank you, our Father,
that your love reaches to the heavens,
and your faithfulness to the skies;
that your justice is like the deep sea.
Your unfailing mercies cannot be bought,
we feast on your goodness
and drink from the river of your blessing;
thank you, through Jesus, your Son, our Lord. **Amen.**

343 THANKSGIVING
Rescue, release, dedication, witness
from Psalm 40

Lord God, you heard my cry
and came to my rescue,
you pulled me from the quicksand
and set me on a rock;
you taught me a new song to sing,
a song of praise to our God:
may others hear it and believe!

Lord, you do not need sacrifices
    or offerings;
for you have given me ears to hear you
and you want me to respond:
'Lord, I come!'

Lord, in the fellowship of your people
I will declare the good news
    of your salvation,
I will tell them how you helped me,
and not be silent about your faithfulness
and your constant love;
through Jesus my redeemer. **Amen.**

344 THANKSGIVING
Church anniversary/dedication, celebration
from Psalm 48

O Lord God,
you are great and most worthy of praise;
worship in your house
is our greatest joy on earth.
You are our God
and will for ever be our guide;
you have done great things from the beginning.
As we have heard, so have we seen:
your name like your praise
reaches to the ends of the earth;
your hand is full of good things.
Now in your presence we recall your unfailing love;
through Jesus our Lord. **Amen.**

345 THANKSGIVING
Harvest
from Psalm 65

Our God,
we come to praise you together,
and to renew our promises to you;
for you have overcome our failings,
you have forgiven our sins
and answered our prayers:
thank you for sending the rain
   to make the land rich and fertile,
thank you for filling the streams with water,
thank you for providing the earth with crops,
for making the young plants grow,
thank you for the cattle in the pastures
and the sheep upon the hillside;
thank you, Lord, for the harvest. **Amen.**

346 THANKSGIVING
New Year, general
from Psalm 92

Thank you,
our Lord and God most high,
for your constant love every morning
and your faithfulness each night,
for all you have done that rejoices our hearts:
you have taught us your wisdom,
you have blessed us in our worship,
you have given us happiness,
you have kept us safe,
you have strengthened us
   through the passing years.
Lord, we trust in your mercy and protection:
thank you, Lord. **Amen.**

347 THANKSGIVING
God's majesty, celebration
from Psalm 97

Lord God,
you are King of the earth;
the whole world rejoices before you.
Clouds and darkness conceal you;
you rule with righteousness and justice.
Fire precedes you – lighting and thunder,
the earth trembles!
Your glory in the skies
    is there for all to see.
Those who worship other gods
    are put to shame,
for you are greater;
your light shines
on those who love you and hate evil.

Lord, you have done wonderful things
and we are glad;
we recall what you have done for us
and we give you thanks;
in Jesus' name. **Amen.**

348 THANKSGIVING
Holy Communion
from Psalm 111

God our Father,
we, the family of your people,
praise you with all our heart:
for great are your works
and wonderful the things you do;
glorious and majestic are your deeds,
and your righteousness is everlasting.

Here we remember what you have done for us –
your grace and your compassion;
you have given, to us who worship you, this food to eat,
and your covenant is for ever –
redemption for your people;
holy and awesome is your name. **Amen.**

349 THANKSGIVING
Epiphany, worldwide church, mission
from Psalm 117

Lord of all the nations,
we your people praise you and extol you;
for your love towards us is great,
and your faithfulness endures for ever. **Amen.**

350 THANKSGIVING
Faith, renewal, Easter
from Psalm 118

God our Father,
we thank you;
for you are good,
and your love endures for ever.
We thank you that you have heard our cry
and set us free;
we thank you that you are with us,
and we need not be afraid;
we thank you that you have answered us,
and become our salvation;
through our Lord Jesus Christ. **Amen.**

351 THANKSGIVING
Creation, Rogation, deliverance
from Psalm 136

God our Father,
we thank you;
for you are good,
and your love endures for ever.
We thank you that you are God of gods
and Lord of lords.
We thank you that you do great wonders;
that in your wisdom you made the skies
    and spread out the earth and sea.
We thank you that you made the lights of heaven –
the sun to rule the day,
and the moon and stars to govern the night.
We thank you that you have remembered us
    in our humanity,
that you have freed us from our enemies
and from the power of evil and death;
through Jesus Christ our Lord. **Amen.**

352 THANKSGIVING
Lent, answered prayer
from Psalm 138

God our Father,
we thank you with all our hearts
and sing to you our songs and hymns;
we bow before you in worship, and praise you,
because you have loved us
and shown yourself faithful.
Your word is mighty like your name,
and when we call to you
you answer our prayer
and give us the strength we need.

Though you are very high,
you care for the lowly,
and the proud cannot hide from you;
when we are surrounded by troubles
you keep us safe.

Father, your love is eternal:
complete in us the work you have begun;
through Jesus our redeemer. **Amen.**

353 THANKSGIVING
Lent, the family, mission
from Psalm 145

God our Father,
gracious and compassionate,
slow to anger and rich in mercy:
we thank you that you keep your promises,
and love all that you have made;
you uphold those who fall,
and lift up those who are bowed low;
you open your hand
and satisfy the desires of your people
   who fear you,
you hear our cry and save us.
Therefore we proclaim your goodness:
let every creature praise your holy name,
for ever and ever. **Amen.**

354 THANKSGIVING
Pentecost, renewal, family, God's word
from Isaiah 59

We thank you, God our Father,
that your arm is strong to save,
and your ear ready to hear;
that, as you promised,
you have come to save your people
   who repent of their sins;
that your Spirit is upon us and will not leave us,
that your word will not depart from us,
nor from our children,
nor from their children
from this time on for ever. **Amen.**

355 THANKSGIVING
Passiontide, God's love and mercy
from Isaiah 63

Our God, we thank you for your kindness
and praise you for your many gracious deeds –
for all the good things you have done for us:
you are our saviour;
in all our trouble you too were troubled,
in your love and mercy you redeemed us;
through Jesus Christ our Lord. **Amen.**

356 THANKSGIVING
Holy Communion
from Matthew 26, Mark 14,
   Luke 22 and I Corinthians 11

Heavenly Father,
we thank you that when the time came
and on the night that he was betrayed,
Jesus ate the Passover meal
   with his disciples;
and while he was eating,
he took bread,
gave thanks to you and broke it.
Then he gave it to them saying,
'This is my body, which is for you.
Do this in remembrance of me.'

In the same way, after supper
he took the cup, gave thanks to you,
and gave it to them all saying,
'This cup is God's new covenant in my blood,
which is poured out for many
for the forgiveness of sins:
do this, whenever you drink it,
in remembrance of me.'

[*Passiontide*:
Then Jesus said,
'I tell you the truth,
I will not drink wine again
until I drink the new wine of the kingdom of God.']

[*Passiontide, Advent, mission*:
This means that every time we eat this bread
and drink from this cup
we proclaim his death until he comes.]

357 THANKSGIVING
Christmas, Epiphany
from Luke 1

We bless you, our Lord God,
that you have come
and have redeemed your people,
raising up for us a strong saviour
  from the family of your servant David,
as you promised through your prophets long ago.
You have rescued us from the grip of our enemy;
you have enabled us to serve you without fear,
in holiness and righteousness before you
  all our days.
We thank you that you have given to us, your people,
  the knowledge of salvation
through the forgiveness of our sins;
and that by your tender mercy
the Sun has risen into heaven
to shine on all who live in darkness
and in the shadow of death,
and to guide our feet into the way of peace. **Amen.**

358 THANKSGIVING
Holy Communion: especially Easter
from Luke 24

Lord Jesus Christ,
we are your disciples
[it is evening,
the day is nearly over,]
and we come to your table.
Our hearts are warmed
for you have talked with us,
   and have opened the Scriptures to us.
Now in your name
we take bread and give thanks,
we break it and receive it:
open our eyes, confirm our faith
   and fill us with joy;
that we may believe, and declare to all:
It is true! The Lord has risen. **Amen.**

359 THANKSGIVING
Pentecost, renewal, healing, witness
from Acts 4

We thank you, Sovereign Lord,
creator of sky, earth and sea,
and everything in them,
that you spoke by your Holy Spirit
through your prophets:
stretch out your hand now to heal,
to perform miraculous signs and wonders –
fill us with your Holy Spirit
that we may speak for you boldly;
through the name of your holy servant, Jesus. **Amen.**

360 THANKSGIVING
Harvest
from Acts 14

Living God,
you made heaven and earth,
the sea,
and everything in them:
we thank you for all your kindness;
for giving us the rain from heaven
and crops in their season –
you provide us with food
and fill our hearts with joy;
thank you, Lord. **Amen.**

361 THANKSGIVING
Giving, study
from Romans 11

Lord God our Father,
thank you for the riches of your wisdom and knowledge:
unsearchable are your judgements;
untraceable your paths.
Who has known your mind or been your counsellor?
Who has ever given anything to you
    that you should repay?
For from you and through you and to you
    are all things:
to you be the glory for ever! **Amen.**

362 THANKSGIVING
Holy Spirit, renewal, rededication
from 1 Corinthians 12

We thank you, our God, for our unity in diversity:
different kinds of gifts
    but the same Spirit;
different kinds of service
    but the same Lord;
different kinds of working
    but the same God,
Father, Son and Holy Spirit. **Amen.**

363 THANKSGIVING
Faith, Passiontide, forgiveness
from Ephesians 1

We praise you,
God and Father of our Lord Jesus,
for you have blessed us from heaven
with every spiritual blessing in Christ;
you chose us in him
    before the creation of the world
to be holy and blameless in your sight.
We thank you for your glorious grace,
freely given in your beloved Son;
by whose blood we are redeemed,
our sins forgiven
    according to the riches of your grace;
for his name's sake. **Amen.**

364 THANKSGIVING
Ascension, worldwide church, mission
from Philippians 2

We praise you, our God,
because you have exalted your Son Jesus Christ
to your right hand in glory,
and given him the name above every name,
that at the name of Jesus every knee should bow.

So, our Father,
accept our worship, our love and thanksgiving;
and grant that we, with those of every tongue,
may confess that Jesus Christ is Lord,
to your glory and honour. **Amen.**

365 THANKSGIVING
Easter, heaven, resurrection
from 1 Peter 1

We thank you, our God,
the Father of our Lord Jesus Christ,
that in your great mercy
you have given us birth into new life and hope
by raising Jesus Christ from death,
and an inheritance in heaven
that can never spoil or fade.

We thank you that, through faith,
you keep us safe by your power
until the coming salvation
ready to be revealed at the end of time:
receive our praise
through the one whom we love
and in whom we believe,
Jesus Christ our Lord. **Amen.**

366 THANKSGIVING
Good Friday, ministry, rededication
from Revelation 1

Jesus Christ,
faithful witness, firstborn from the dead,
ruler of the powers of this world:
we thank you that you love us
and by your sacrificial death
have freed us from our sins
and made us a kingdom of priests
to serve our God and Father:
to you, Lord Jesus,
be glory and power for ever and ever! **Amen.**

367 THANKSGIVING
All Saints
from Revelation 2 and 3

Hear the promises of Jesus,
the first and the last, the living one,
who was dead but now is alive for ever and ever,
who has authority over death
  and the world of the dead:

Those who win the victory
will eat from the tree of life:
thank you, Lord Jesus.

Those who win the victory
will not be hurt by the second death:
thank you, Lord Jesus.

Those who win the victory
will be given a new name:
thank you, Lord Jesus.

Those who win the victory
will receive authority from the Father:
thank you, Lord Jesus.

Those who win the victory
will be clothed in white,
and their names will remain
  in the book of the living:
thank you, Lord Jesus. Amen.

ACCLAMATION

368 ACCLAMATION
Ascension, God's majesty, God's people
from Exodus 15

Who is like you, Lord our God –
majestic in holiness,
awesome in glory,
working wonders?

In your unfailing love
you will lead your redeemed:
in your strength you will guide us.

To you we sing,
for you are highly exalted:
you will reign for ever and ever. Amen.

369 ACCLAMATION
Lent, obedience, discipleship
from Deuteronomy 10

Our Lord God,
we want to fear you,
to walk in your ways,
to love and serve you with all our heart
    and all our soul,
and to obey your commandments;
for you are God of gods and Lord of lords,
the great one, mighty and awesome:
you are our God,
and we will praise you for ever. Amen.

370 ACCLAMATION
Giving, church anniversary, dedication
from 1 Chronicles 29

Lord God,
may you be praised for ever and ever:
you are great and powerful,
glorious, splendid and majestic;
everything in heaven and earth is yours,
and you are king,
supreme ruler over all:
all riches and wealth come from you;
you rule everything
by your strength and power;
you alone are able to make anyone
    great and strong:
now, our God, we give you thanks
and praise your glorious name. Amen.

371 ACCLAMATION
Giving, church anniversary, dedication
from 1 Chronicles 29 (alternative)

Yours, Lord, is the greatness,
the power, the glory, the splendour and the majesty:
everything in heaven and on earth is yours.

Everything comes from you:
and of your own do we give you.

372 ACCLAMATION
Creation, majesty of God
from Nehemiah 9

Blessed be your glorious name, O Lord our God,
may it be exalted
above all human worship and praise:
you alone are the Lord,
you made the skies and the universe beyond,
you made the earth and all that is upon it,
the sea and all that is in it;
you give life to everything –
you are the Lord our God:
with the hosts of heaven we worship you. Amen.

373 ACCLAMATION
Advent, celebration, general
from Isaiah 25

O Lord,
we exalt and praise your name,
for you are faithful to us
and have done marvellous things –
things promised long ago.
You are our God:
we trust in you, and you save us;
through Jesus our redeemer. Amen.

374 ACCLAMATION
Easter, resurrection
from 1 Peter 1

Praise be to you, God our Father:
for, in your great mercy,
you have given us new birth
   into a living hope,
through the resurrection from the dead
of Jesus Christ our Lord. **Amen.**

375 ACCLAMATION
New Year, holiness, world church
from Revelation 15

Great and marvellous are your deeds,
   Lord God almighty;
just and true are your ways,
   King of the ages.
Who will not fear you, O Lord,
and bring glory to your name?
For you alone are holy;
all nations will come and worship before you,
for your righteous acts have been revealed. **Amen.**

376 ACCLAMATION
Justice, God's majesty
from Revelation 15 (variant)

Lord God almighty,
what you have done is great and wonderful.
King of the ages,
just and true are your ways;
we stand in awe of you,
we declare your greatness:
you alone are holy. **Amen.**

DOXOLOGY/ASCRIPTION

377 DOXOLOGY
Creation, God's majesty, church anniversary
from Psalm 29

O Lord, holy One,
with all the hosts of heaven
we praise your glory and power
and bow down to worship you.
We hear your voice in the thunder,
in all its power and majesty;
we perceive your strength
   in the mighty forests
and upon the jagged mountains.
We sense your presence
   in the lightning flash
and the rumbling earthquake;
you rule over the deep sea
   as king for ever,
you give strength to your people
and bless them with peace.
And in your house everyone shouts:
'Glory to God! Amen'.

378 DOXOLOGY
Worship, church anniversary, flower festival
From Psalm 63

Lord God, our God,
we have seen you in the sanctuary,
we have looked on your power and your glory.
Because your love is better than life
our lips will glorify you,
we will praise you as long as we live,
and in your name we will lift up our hearts;
through Jesus Christ our Lord. **Amen**.

379 DOXOLOGY
Majesty of God, Advent, judgement
from Isaiah 23 and 24

Lord almighty,
you bring low all pride and glory
and humble those who are renowned in the earth,
you stretch out your hand over the sea
and make the nations tremble.
To you we raise our voices,
and shout for joy;
we acclaim your majesty,
we give you praise,
we exalt your name.
From the ends of the earth we sing:
'Glory to the righteous One!'
for you will reign among us for ever and ever. **Amen.**

380 DOXOLOGY
God's wisdom, study, general
from Romans 11

Our Lord God,
how profound are the riches
of your wisdom and knowledge;
how unsearchable your judgements,
and your paths beyond tracing out!
Who has known your mind,
who has been your counsellor;
who has ever given to you,
that you should repay?
For from you and through you and to you
are all things:
yours be the glory for ever! Amen.

381 DOXOLOGY
Conference, study, God's wisdom
from Romans 11 (variant)

Lord God our Father,
how great are the riches
   of your wisdom and your knowledge;
how unsearchable your judgements
and your paths beyond discovering;
from you and through you and to you
   are all things:
to you be glory for ever! **Amen.**

382 DOXOLOGY/ASCRIPTION
Guidance, God's wisdom
from Romans 11 (alternative)

To the God of all wisdom and knowledge
whose judgements are unsearchable
and paths beyond understanding,
be glory for ever and ever. **Amen.**

383 DOXOLOGY/ASCRIPTION
Mission, evangelism
from Romans 16

To God who has the power
to make us strong in the Gospel
to proclaim Jesus Christ,
to him be glory for ever and ever. **Amen.**

384 DOXOLOGY/ASCRIPTION
God's wisdom, study, general
from Romans 16

Glory to God
who alone is all-wise;
through Jesus Christ for ever! **Amen.**

385 DOXOLOGY/ASCRIPTION
Passiontide
from Galatians 1

To God our Father
and the Lord Jesus Christ,
who gave himself for our sins
to rescue us from this present evil age,
according to the will of our God and Father,
be glory for ever and ever. **Amen.**

386 DOXOLOGY/ASCRIPTION
Faith, renewal, church anniversary
from Ephesians 3

Now to God the Father,
who is able to do
immeasurably more than all we ask or think,
by the power of the Spirit at work in us:
to him be glory in the Church
and in Christ Jesus
throughout all generations
for ever and ever! Amen.

387 DOXOLOGY/ASCRIPTION
Answered prayer, general
from Philippians 4

To our God and Father,
who meets all our needs
according to his glorious riches
in Christ Jesus,
be glory for ever and ever. **Amen.**

388 DOXOLOGY/ASCRIPTION
God's majesty
from 1 Timothy 1

Now to the king eternal,
immortal, invisible,
the only God,
be honour and glory
for ever and ever. **Amen.**

389 DOXOLOGY/ASCRIPTION
God's majesty, civic
from 1 Timothy 6

To God,
the blessed and only Ruler,
the King of kings and Lord of lords,
who alone is immortal
and who lives in unapproachable light:
to him be honour and might for ever. Amen.

390 DOXOLOGY/ASCRIPTION
Mission, evangelism
from 2 Timothy 4

To the Lord,
who stands at our side
and gives us strength
to proclaim the good news
that all may hear,
be glory for ever and ever. **Amen.**

391 DOXOLOGY/ASCRIPTION
Temptation, deliverance
from 2 Timothy 1

To the Lord
who rescues us from every evil attack
and will bring us safely
   to his heavenly kingdom,
be glory for ever and ever. **Amen.**

392 DOXOLOGY/ASCRIPTION
Easter, Jesus as Shepherd
from Hebrews 13

To our Lord Jesus,
risen from the dead,
that great shepherd of the sheep,
be glory for ever and ever. **Amen.**

393 DOXOLOGY/ASCRIPTION
People of God, calling
from 1 Peter 5

To the God of all grace,
who called us to his eternal glory in Christ,
be the power for ever and ever. **Amen.**

394 DOXOLOGY/ASCRIPTION
Passiontide, Ascension, general
from 2 Peter 3

To our Lord and saviour Jesus Christ,
be glory both now and for ever. **Amen.**

395 DOXOLOGY/ASCRIPTION
Lent, temptation, All Saints
from Jude

Now to him who is able to keep us from falling,
and to present us
before the presence of his glory
without fault and with great joy;
to the only wise God, our Saviour:
be glory and majesty, dominion and power,
both now and for ever. Amen.

396 DOXOLOGY/ASCRIPTION
Passiontide, church, ministry
from Revelation 1

To him who loves us,
and has freed us from our sins by his blood,
and has made us to be a kingdom and priests
to serve his God and Father:
to him be glory and power,
for ever and ever. Amen.

397 DOXOLOGY
Good Friday, worldwide church
from Revelation 4 and 5

You are worthy, Lord our God,
to receive glory and honour and power;
for you created all things:
and by your will they existed
and were created.

You are worthy, O Christ,
for you were slain,
and by your blood you ransomed us for God;
from every tribe and tongue
and people and nation,
you made us a kingdom of priests
to serve our God.

To him who sits upon the throne,
and to the Lamb,
be blessing and honour
and glory and might
for ever and ever. **Amen.**

398 DOXOLOGY
Passiontide, church, ministry
from Revelation 4 and 5 (alternative)

You are worthy, Lord our God,
to receive glory and honour and power:
for you created all things,
and by your will they existed
and were created.

You are worthy, O Christ,
for you were slain,
and by your blood you ransomed us for God:
from every tribe and tongue and people and nation,
you made us a kingdom of priests
to serve our God.

To him who sits upon the throne,
and to the Lamb,
be blessing and honour
and glory and might
for ever and ever. Amen.

399 DOXOLOGY
Worldwide church, mission, ministry
from Revelation 4 and 5 (alternative)

O Lord our God,
you are worthy, to receive glory, honour, and power;
for you created all things,
and by your will
they were given existence and life:
Glory to God in the highest!

O Lamb of God,
you are worthy to receive wisdom,
    strength, and praise,
for by your death you bought for God,
people of every tribe, language, nation and race:
Glory to God in the highest!

You have made them a kingdom of priests
to serve our God,
and they shall rule on earth:
Glory to God in the highest!

To him who sits upon the throne
and to the Lamb,
be praise and honour, glory and power,
for ever and ever! Amen.

400 DOXOLOGY
Trinity, God's majesty, dedication, worship
from Revelation 15

Glory be to you, our God,
Father, Son, and Holy Spirit:
you have power, wisdom and majesty –
receive from us
honour, glory, worship and blessing.
Great and marvellous are your works,
just and true are your ways:
worthy is your name for ever! Amen.

401 DOXOLOGY

Trinity, God's majesty, dedication, worship
from Revelation 15

Glory be to you, our God,
Father, Son, and Holy Spirit!
You have power, wisdom and majesty:
receive from us
honour, glory, worship and blessing.

Great and marvellous are your works,
just and true are your ways:
blessing and honour and glory and power
to him who reigns upon the throne,
and to the Lamb,
through the one eternal Spirit,
now and for ever. Amen.

BLESSING

402 BLESSING
People of God, forgiveness, protection
from Exodus 33

God almighty,
who has revealed his goodness to *you*
and proclaimed his name among *you,*
show *you* his glory.

The Lord of compassion, have mercy on *you,*
the Lord who forgives *your* sins
hide *you* in the cleft of the Rock
and cover *you* with his hand;
the presence of the Lord
who knows *you* by name
and in whose sight *you* have found favour,
go with *you* now
and give *you* rest. **Amen.**

403 BLESSING
Prayer, general
from Numbers 6

The Lord bless *you* and keep *you;*
the Lord make his face to smile upon *you*
and be gracious to *you;*
the Lord turn towards *you*
and give *you* peace. **Amen.**

404 BLESSING
General
from Numbers 6 (variant)

The Lord bless *you* and take care of *you,*
the Lord be kind and gracious to *you,*
the Lord look on *you* with favour
and give *you* peace. **Amen.**

405 BLESSING
General
from Numbers 6 (traditional)

The Lord bless *you* and keep *you*,
the Lord make his face to shine upon *you*
and be gracious to *you*,
the Lord lift up his countenance upon *you*
and give *you* peace;
and the blessing of God the Father, Son
   and Holy Spirit
be among *you*
and remain with *you* always. **Amen.**

406 BLESSING
Prayer, general
from Numbers 6 (alternative)

The Lord bless *you* and watch over *you*,
the Lord make his face to shine upon *you*
and be gracious to *you*,
the Lord look kindly on *you*
and give *you* peace;
and the blessing of God almighty,
the Father, the Son, and the Holy Spirit,
be among *you* and remain with *you* always. **Amen.**

407 BLESSING
Lent, ministry, general
from Deuteronomy 10

Fear the Lord your God,
walk in his ways,
love him with all your heart,
serve him with all your soul,
obey his commandments;
and the blessing of God almighty,
the Father, the Son and the Holy Spirit
be with you always. **Amen.**

408 BLESSING
Rogation, general
from Deuteronomy 28

The Lord our God
open his storehouse of heaven
and send his blessing on *our* land:
bless *us* in the city,
bless *us* in the country;
bless *our* homes with children;
bless *our* farms with crops,
   our orchards with fruit;
bless *our* industry with produce,
   our commerce with trade;
bless *us* in *our* going out and coming in;
bless *us* in obedience to his will,
grant *us* his prosperity,
and lead *us* to follow him alone for ever. **Amen.**

409 BLESSING
Lent, obedience, general
from Joshua 1

Be strong and courageous,
be careful to observe
God's commandments –
remember them, speak of them, obey them;
do not be fearful, do not be discouraged;
and the Lord your God be with you
wherever you go. **Amen.**

410 BLESSING
Lent, obedience, general
from Joshua 1 (alternative)

Let us be strong and courageous,
careful to observe God's commandments;
to remember them, to speak of them
   and to obey them.
Let us not be fearful,
nor let us be discouraged;
and may the Lord our God be with us
wherever we go. **Amen.**

411 BLESSING
Prayer, evening, general
from 1 Kings 8

The Lord *your* God be with *you*,
never to leave *you*
or forsake *you*;
the Lord turn *your* heart to him,
to walk in his ways
and to keep his commandments;
the words *you* pray before the Lord
be near him day and night;
and the blessing of God the Father,
God the Son, and God the Holy Spirit
be with *you* always. **Amen.**

412 BLESSING   PGIMF May 2005
Creation
from Psalm 8

God who made the heavens,
who set the moon and stars in place,
who crowns *you* with glory and honour,
making *you* to rule over the works of his hands,
whose name is majestic in all the earth;
the Father, the Son and the Holy Spirit,
grant *you* his blessing evermore. **Amen.**

413 BLESSING
Creation, God's word
from Psalm 19

God, whose glory the heavens declare,
whose handiwork the skies proclaim,
who speaks through his creation:
revive *your* spirit with his word,
make *you* wise by his laws
and give *you* joy through his commands;
now and for ever. **Amen.**

414 BLESSING
Prayer, dedication, commissioning
from Psalm 20

The Lord answer *you* when *you* are in distress,
the God of mercy protect *you*,
the Lord accept the offering of *your* life
and receive *your* prayers,
the Lord give *you* the desires of *your* heart,
and make all *your* plans succeed;
the Lord make others rejoice in *you*,
to the praise of his holy name.
And the blessing of our God,
who is able to keep us from falling
and to raise us up victorious,
be upon *you* and remain with *you* always. **Amen.**

415 BLESSING
Ministry, service, obedience, God's love
from Psalm 33

The Lord
in his faithfulness
watch over you:
obey him,
wait for him,
rejoice in him;
and his unfailing love
be upon you always. **Amen.**

416 BLESSING
Ministry, service, obedience, God's love
from Psalm 33 (alternative)

May the Lord
in his faithfulness
watch over us:
let us obey him,
wait for him,
rejoice in him;
and his unfailing love
be upon us always. **Amen.**

417 BLESSING
God's love, patience, faith
from Psalm 33

Wait for the Lord in hope –
he is your help and shield;
rejoice your heart in him,
trust his holy name:
and his unfailing love rest upon you
as you put your hope in him. **Amen.**

418 BLESSING
God's love, patience, faith
from Psalm 33 (alternative)

Let us wait for the Lord in hope –
he is our help and shield;
let us rejoice our hearts in him
and trust his holy name.
May his unfailing love rest upon us
as we put our hope in him. **Amen.**

419 BLESSING
Faith, prayer, healing
from Psalm 33 (variant)

Wait for the Lord in hope,
for he is your help and your shield;
let your heart rejoice in him
and trust his holy name:
may his unfailing love rest upon you
as you put your hope in him;
and the blessing of God almighty,
the Father, the Son and the Holy Spirit
be with *you* always. **Amen.**

420 BLESSING
Commitment/dedication, trust
from Psalm 37

Trust the Lord and do right,
find in him your happiness
   and your heart's desire,
give yourself to him,
wait patiently for him;
and the Lord God almighty
bring you prosperity and peace. **Amen.**

421 BLESSING
Commitment/dedication, trust
from Psalm 37 (alternative)

Let us trust in the Lord and do right,
finding in him our happiness
    and our heart's desire;
let us give ourselves to him
and wait for him in patience;
and may the Lord God almighty
bring us prosperity and peace. **Amen.**

422 BLESSING
In times of trouble/opposition
from Psalm 46

God is your strength and shield,
always ready to help in time of trouble:
so do not be afraid
but see what he has done:
and the Lord God almighty,
Father, Son and Holy Spirit,
be with you evermore. **Amen.**

423 BLESSING
Study, God's love, obedience
from Psalm 86

Be taught by the Lord,
obey him faithfully,
serve him with complete devotion,
praise him with all your heart,
proclaim his greatness
   and his constant love;
and the blessing of God almighty,
the Father, the Son and the Holy Spirit,
be with you always. **Amen.**

424 BLESSING
Study, God's love, obedience
from Psalm 86 (alternative)

Let us be taught by the Lord,
faithful in our obedience,
serving him with complete devotion,
praising him with all our heart,
proclaiming his greatness
   and his constant love;
and the blessing of God almighty,
the Father, the Son and the Holy Spirit,
be with us always. **Amen.**

425 BLESSING
Prayer, forgiveness, general
from Psalm 10

The Lord hear *your* prayer
and listen to *your* cry for mercy;
the Lord turn his face towards *you*
and answer *you* quickly in *your* distress;
the Lord arise and take pity on *you*,
the Lord show *you* his compassion;
the Lord strengthen *you*,
and reveal to *you* his glory;
the Lord look down from heaven
    and bring *you* peace. **Amen.**

426 BLESSING
Social responsibility, parents
from Psalm 115

The Lord who regards all –
humble and great alike,
bless you that fear him;
the Lord prosper your way,
the Lord bless your children;
the Lord, the maker of heaven and earth,
bless you both now and evermore. **Amen.**

427 BLESSING
Social responsibility, parents,
from Psalm 115 (alternative)

The Lord who regards all –
humble and great alike,
bless us who fear him;
the Lord prosper our way,
the Lord bless our children;
the Lord, the maker of heaven and earth,
bless us now and evermore. **Amen.**

428 BLESSING
Witness, obedience
from Psalm 119 (41–48)

Obey the Lord because you love him;
trust his word,
that you may be able to answer
   those who reproach you;
do not be ashamed to proclaim his truth,
think about him always,
respect and love his commandments:
and the blessing of God the Father,
   God the Son, and God the Holy Spirit,
be upon you. **Amen.**

429 BLESSING
Witness, obedience
from Psalm 119 (41–48, alternative)

Let us obey the Lord
because we love him;
let us trust his word,
that we may be able to answer
    those who reproach us;
let us not be ashamed to proclaim his truth;
let us think about him always,
and obey his commandments:
and the blessing of God the Father,
    God the Son, and God the Holy Spirit
be upon us always. **Amen.**

430 BLESSING
Providence, protection
from Psalm 121

The Lord,
who made heaven and earth,
watch over *you*,
the Lord stay close by *your* side,
the Lord guard *your* life
    and keep *you* from harm,
the Lord protect *you* as *you* come and go,
and bless *you* now and evermore. **Amen.**

431 BLESSING
Family, marriage
from Psalm 128

The Lord bless *you* all the days of your life:
may *you* have prosperity;
may *you* live to see *your* children's children:
and the love of God,
the Father, Son and Holy Spirit
enrich *you* always. **Amen.**

432 BLESSING
Civic, visitors present
from Psalm 129

The blessing of the Lord be upon you:
we bless you in the name of our God,
Father, Son and Holy Spirit. **Amen.**

433 BLESSING
Church dedication, anniversary, worship
from Psalm 134

The Lord,
the maker of heaven and earth,
bless *you*
who lift up *your* hands in his presence
and praise him;
the Lord bless *you* from this holy place
and wherever *you* may go;
the blessing of God almighty,
Father, Son and Holy Spirit,
be upon *you* for ever and ever. **Amen.**

434 BLESSING
Baptism, confirmation, commissioning
from Isaiah 11

The spirit of the Lord rest upon *you*:
the spirit of wisdom and understanding,
the spirit of counsel and power,
the spirit of knowledge and the fear of the Lord;
that *you* may delight in the Lord,
now and always. **Amen.**

435 BLESSING
Advent, All Saints
from Isaiah 35

Strengthen the feeble hands,
steady the knees that give way;
behold the glory of the Lord,
the splendour of our God!
Be strong, do not fear –
your God will come:
his blessing be upon *you*
     now and always. **Amen.**

436 BLESSING
Trust, prayer, evening, renewal
from Isaiah 26

Trust in the Lord,
your eternal Rock,
and he will keep your minds in perfect peace.
Keep faith with him,
walk with him, wait for him, desire him;
reach out to him in the night,
seek him in the morning:
and his blessing be upon you always. **Amen.**

437 BLESSING
Trust, prayer, evening, renewal,
from Isaiah 26 (alternative)

Let us trust in the Lord,
our eternal Rock,
that he may keep our minds in perfect peace.
Let us keep faith with him,
walk with him, wait for him, desire him;
reach out to him in the night,
seek him in the morning:
and his blessing be upon us always. **Amen.**

438 BLESSING
Easter, God's love, healing
from Isaiah 40

The Lord *your* Shepherd tenderly care for *you*,
gather *you* in his arms,
carry *you* close to his heart
and gently lead *you*;
and the blessing of God the Father,
   God the Son, and God the Holy Spirit,
be with *you* always. **Amen.**

439 BLESSING
Forgiveness, healing and renewal
from Isaiah 57

The Lord guide *you* and restore his comfort to *you*;
the Lord bring praise to *your* lips;
the Lord send *you* peace wherever *you* go;
the Lord in his mercy heal *you*:
and the blessing of God almighty,
the Father, the Son and the Holy Spirit,
be with *you* now and always. **Amen.**

440 BLESSING
Forgiveness, healing
from Isaiah 57

The Lord look upon *your* need and heal *you;*
the Lord guide *you,*
the Lord restore comfort to *you,*
the Lord give *you* his peace. **Amen.**

441 BLESSING
Evangelism, ministry
from Isaiah 61

The Sovereign Lord
anoint you with his blessing:
preach good news to the poor,
go and bind up the broken-hearted,
proclaim freedom for the captives
    and release for those who are in darkness,
declare the Lord's favour and his judgement,
comfort all who mourn;
and the grace of our God,
Father, Son and Holy Spirit,
be upon you always. **Amen.**

442 BLESSING

Evangelism, ministry
from Isaiah 61 (alternative)

The Sovereign Lord
anoint us with his blessing
that we may preach good news to the poor,
go and bind up the broken-hearted,
proclaim freedom for the captives,
and release for those who are in darkness;
that we may declare the Lord's favour
    and his judgement
and comfort those who mourn;
and the grace of our God,
Father, Son and Holy Spirit,
be upon us always. **Amen.**

443 BLESSING

Evangelism, mission, ministry, commissioning
from Matthew 28

At the word of Christ,
and by the authority given to him
    in heaven and on earth,
go and make disciples of all people,
in the name of the Father, of the Son
    and of the Holy Spirit;
and the presence of Christ be with you
everywhere and always. **Amen.**

444 BLESSING
Evangelism, mission, ministry, commissioning
from Matthew 28 (alternative)

At the word of Christ,
and by the authority given to him
  in heaven and on earth,
let us go and make disciples of all people,
in the name of the Father, of the Son
  and of the Holy Spirit;
and may Christ's presence be with us
everywhere and always. **Amen.**

445 BLESSING
Peace, opposition
from John 14

Jesus said,
'Peace I leave with you: my peace I give to you.
Do not let your heart be troubled or afraid'.
The peace of God,
Father, Son and Holy Spirit,
be upon *you* and remain with *you* for ever. **Amen.**

446 BLESSING
Pentecost, renewal, church, fellowship
from John 15

Remain in Jesus Christ,
obey his commands,
bear much fruit,
love one another;
and the blessing of God the Father,
  God the Son and God the Holy Spirit,
be with you always. **Amen.**

447 BLESSING
Pentecost, renewal, church, fellowship
from John 15 (alternative)

Let us remain in Jesus Christ,
and obey his commands
to bear much fruit
and to love one another;
so may the blessing of God the Father,
  God the Son and God the Holy Spirit,
be with us always. **Amen.**

448 BLESSING
Commissioning, music, God's peace
from Acts 2

The Lord be near *you* at all times,
the Lord walk beside *you*
  so that *you* will not be troubled,
the Lord fill *your* heart with gladness,
and *your* mouth with joyful songs;
and the blessing of God almighty,
the Father, the Son and the Holy Spirit,
be with *you* always. **Amen.**

449 BLESSING
Creation
from Romans 1

God, whose invisible qualities –
his eternal power and divine nature,
are clearly seen in his creation
since the beginning,
grant *you* to know his righteousness
in Christ Jesus,
and his eternal peace,
and to enjoy the works of his hands:
and the blessing of Father, Son
    and Holy Spirit,
one God, be with *you* always. **Amen.**

450 BLESSING
Easter, baptism, funeral, obedience
from Romans 14

Christ our saviour,
the Lord of the living and the dead,
who died and rose again to life,
grant that in life *you* may live for him alone,
and in dying belong to him for ever. **Amen.**

451 BLESSING
Unity
from Romans 15

The God of strength and encouragement
grant *you* to live in such harmony with each other,
that together *you* may with one voice glorify
the God and Father of our Lord Jesus Christ;
and the blessing of God the Father, God the Son,
    and God the Holy Spirit
be with *you* always. **Amen.**

452 BLESSING
Unity, fellowship
from Romans 15 (variant)

The God of patience and encouragement
give *you* a spirit of unity among *yourselves*
as *you* follow Christ Jesus,
that with one mind and one mouth
you may glorify the God and Father
 of our Lord Jesus Christ;
and the blessing of God almighty,
the Father, the Son and the Holy Spirit,
be with *you* always. **Amen.**

453 BLESSING
Joy, peace, faith, renewal
from Romans 15

The God of hope
fill *you* with all joy and peace
as *you* trust in him,
so that *you* may overflow with hope;
through the power of the Holy Spirit. **Amen.**

454 BLESSING
Ministry, commissioning, renewal
from Romans 15

By our Lord Jesus Christ,
and by the love the Spirit gives,
pray fervently to God for your leaders:
and may God, our source of peace,
be with you all. **Amen.**

455 BLESSING
All Saints, testing, courage
from 1 Corinthians 16

Be on your guard,
stand firm in the faith,
be people of courage,
be strong,
do everything in love;
and the grace of the Lord Jesus
    be with you always. **Amen.**

456 BLESSING
All Saints, courage, testing
from 1 Corinthians 16 (alternative)

Let us be on our guard,
let us stand firm in the faith,
people of courage,
strong, doing everything in love;
and the grace of the Lord Jesus
    be with us always. **Amen.**

457 BLESSING
Under pressure, in distress
from 2 Corinthians 1

The God and Father of our Lord Jesus Christ –
the Father of compassion and God of all comfort:
comfort *you* in all *your* troubles,
so that *you* can comfort others who are in trouble
with the comfort *you yourselves* have received from him;
and the blessing of God almighty,
the Father, the Son and the Holy Spirit,
be with *you* and remain with *you* always. **Amen.**

458 BLESSING
Easter, testing
from 2 Corinthians 1

Trust the God who raises the dead
to save you from mortal danger,
place your hope in him;
and may he bless you
in answer to your prayer,
so that you may give thanks to him;
through Jesus Christ our Lord. **Amen.**

459 BLESSING
Easter, testing
from 2 Corinthians 1 (alternative)

Let us trust God, who raises the dead,
to save us from mortal danger;
let us place our hope in him:
and may God bless us
in answer to our prayer,
that we may give thanks to him;
through Jesus Christ our Lord. **Amen.**

460 BLESSING
Transfiguration, renewal
from 2 Corinthians 3

Fix your gaze with face unveiled
upon the glory of the Lord,
and be transfigured into his likeness
from one degree of glory to another:
the Spirit of the Lord
    work this miracle in you;
and the blessing of God almighty,
Father, Son and Holy Spirit,
be upon you always. **Amen.**

461 BLESSING

Transfiguration, renewal
from 2 Corinthians 3 (alternative)

Let us fix our gaze with face unveiled
upon the glory of the Lord,
and be transformed into his likeness
from one degree of glory to another:
may the Spirit of the Lord
　　work this miracle in us;
and the blessing of God almighty,
Father, Son and Holy Spirit,
be among us always. **Amen.**

462 BLESSING

Renewal, time of trial, eternal life
from 2 Corinthians 4

Never be discouraged
even though your world decay;
be renewed in spirit day by day,
looking forward
　　to tremendous and eternal glory
fixing your heart on your unseen home
　　which will last for ever;
and the blessing of God,
　　who has created you for heaven
and in token has given you his Spirit,
be upon you now and always. **Amen.**

463 BLESSING
Renewal, time of trial, eternal life
from 2 Corinthians 4 (alternative)

Let us never be discouraged –
even though our world decays,
but, renewed in spirit day by day,
let us look forward
    to tremendous and eternal glory,
fixing our hearts on our unseen home
    which will last for ever;
and the blessing of God,
    who has created us for heaven
and in token has given us his Spirit,
be upon us now and always. **Amen.**

464 BLESSING
Ministry, evangelism
from 2 Corinthians 6

Show yourselves to be God's servants
    through the Holy Spirit;
by your purity, knowledge,
    patience and kindness,
by your genuine love,
by your message of truth
and by the power of God;
and the blessing of the Father,
    the Son and the Holy Spirit
be with you always. **Amen.**

465 BLESSING
Ministry, evangelism
from 2 Corinthians 6 (alternative)

Let us show ourselves to be God's servants
   through the Holy Spirit;
by purity, knowledge, patience and kindness,
by our genuine love,
by our message of truth
and by the power of God;
and the blessing of God the Father,
   God the Son and God the Holy Spirit
be with us always. **Amen.**

466 BLESSING
Lent, renewal
from 2 Corinthians 6

Purify yourselves
from everything that makes the soul unclean,
and be completely holy
by living in awe of God;
and blessing from the Father, the Son
   and the Holy Spirit
be upon you. **Amen.**

467 BLESSING
Lent, renewal
from 2 Corinthians 6 (alternative)

Let us purify ourselves
from everything that makes the soul unclean,
and be completely holy
by living in awe of God;
and blessing from the Father, the Son
   and the Holy Spirit
be upon us always. **Amen.**

468 BLESSING
Unity, service, harmony
from 2 Corinthians 13

Strive for perfection,
listen to wisdom,
agree with one another,
live in peace;
and the God of love and peace
be with you always. **Amen.**

469 BLESSING
Unity, service, harmony
from 2 Corinthians 13 (alternative)

Let us strive for perfection,
listen to wisdom,
agree with one another
and live in peace;
and may the God of love and peace
be with us always. **Amen.**

470 BLESSING
Unity, harmony
from 2 Corinthians 13

Be of one mind,
live in peace;
and the God of love and peace
  be with you always. **Amen.**

471 BLESSING
Unity, harmony
from 2 Corinthians 13 (alternative)

Let us be of one mind
and live in peace;
and the God of love and peace
   be with us always. **Amen.**

472 BLESSING
Fellowship, general
from 2 Corinthians 13

The grace of the Lord Jesus Christ,
and the love of God,
and the fellowship of the Holy Spirit
be with *you* all. **Amen.**

473 BLESSING
Pentecost, renewal, maturity
from Ephesians 1

God,
the glorious Father of our Lord Jesus Christ,
give *you* the Spirit
to make *you* wise and reveal Christ to *you*,
so that *you* may know him better;
the eyes of *your* heart be opened to see his light,
to know:
   the hope to which he has called *you*,
   the riches of glory he promises to his people,
   his power available to all who believe;
and the blessing of God almighty,
the Father, the Son and the Holy Spirit
be among *you* and remain with *you* always. **Amen.**

474 BLESSING
Faith, All Saints, God's love
from Ephesians 3

God,
from the wealth of his glory
give *you* power through his Spirit
to be inwardly strong.
Christ make his home in *your* hearts
  through faith:
that *you* may come to know
how broad, how long,
how high and how deep
  is his love
and be filled with the very nature of God,
Father, Son and Holy Spirit. **Amen.**

475 BLESSING
Pentecost, renewal, musical event
from Ephesians 5

Be filled with the Spirit;
speak to one another
  with psalms, hymns and spiritual songs –
sing and make music in your hearts to the Lord;
and the blessing of God almighty,
the Father, the Son and the Holy Spirit
be with you always. **Amen.**

476 BLESSING
Pentecost, renewal, musical event
from Ephesians 5 (alternative)

Let us be filled with the Spirit,
speaking to one another
    with psalms, hymns and spiritual songs,
singing and making music in our hearts to the Lord;
and the blessing of God almighty,
the Father, the Son and the Holy Spirit,
be with us always. **Amen.**

477 BLESSING
Visiting, unity
from Ephesians 6

Peace be to *you*
and love with faith,
from God the Father and the Lord Jesus Christ;
grace be with all those
who love our Lord Jesus Christ in sincerity;
and the blessing of God almighty,
Father, Son and Holy Spirit,
follow *you* for ever. **Amen.**

478 BLESSING
People of God, witness, prayer
from Philippians 4

Rejoice in the Lord always,
show gentleness to all,
do not be anxious,
make your needs known to God
    by prayer, with thanksgiving;
and the peace of God
guard your heart and mind
    in Christ Jesus. **Amen.**

479 BLESSING
People of God, witness, prayer
from Philippians 4 (alternative)

Let us rejoice in the Lord always,
showing gentleness to all,
not being anxious for anything,
making our needs known to God
    by prayer, with thanksgiving;
and may God's peace
guard our hearts and minds
    in Christ Jesus. **Amen.**

480 BLESSING
Prayer, witness
from Philippians 4 (variant)

Rejoice in the Lord,
let everyone know your gentleness,
do not be anxious,
make your needs known to God;
and the peace of God
    guard you always. **Amen.**

481 BLESSING
Lent, discipline, general
from Philippians 4

Whatever is true, whatever is honourable,
whatever is just, whatever is pure,
whatever is lovely, whatever is gracious;
if there is anything excellent,
or anything worthy of praise:
think on these things;
and the God of peace be with you always. **Amen.**

482 BLESSING
Lent, discipline, general
from Philippians 4 (alternative)

Whatever is true, whatever is honourable,
whatever is just, whatever is pure,
whatever is lovely, whatever is gracious;
if there is anything excellent,
or anything worthy of praise:
let us think on these things;
and the God of peace be with us always. **Amen.**

483 BLESSING
Guidance, maturity, general
from Colossians 1

God the Father fill *you* with the knowledge of his will,
his Spirit give *you* wisdom and understanding,
Christ strengthen *you* with his glorious power
so that *you* may be able to endure, to be patient,
and to give thanks to God with joy in *your* heart;
and the blessing of God almighty,
the Father, the Son, and the Holy Spirit,
be with *you* always. **Amen.**

484 BLESSING
Ascension, ambition, obedience
from Colossians 3

Set your heart on things above,
where Christ is seated at the right hand of God;
and the blessing of God almighty,
the Father, the Son and the Holy Spirit,
be with you always. **Amen.**

485 BLESSING
Ascension, ambition, obedience
from Colossians 3 (alternative)

Let us set our hearts on things above
where Christ is seated at the right hand of God;
and the blessing of God almighty,
the Father, the Son and the Holy Spirit
be with us always. **Amen.**

486 BLESSING
Forgiveness, love, awareness, witness
from Colossians 3

Forgive each other
    as the Lord has forgiven you;
above all virtues put on love;
let the peace of Christ rule your heart,
and be thankful;
and the blessing of God almighty,
the Father, the Son and the Holy Spirit,
be with you always. **Amen.**

487 BLESSING
Forgiveness, love, awareness, witness
from Colossians 3 (alternative)

Let us forgive each other
    as the Lord has forgiven us;
above all virtues let us put on love,
may God's peace rule our hearts
and let us be thankful.
And the blessing of God almighty,
Father, Son and Holy Spirit,
be with us always. **Amen.**

488 BLESSING
Devotion, witness
from Colossians 3

Let the peace of Christ rule your heart,
let the word of Christ dwell in you richly;
whatever you do in word or deed
do all in the name of the Lord Jesus:
and the blessing of God almighty,
the Father, the Son and the Holy Spirit,
be with you always. **Amen.**

489 BLESSING
Devotion, witness
from Colossians 3 (alternative)

May the peace of Christ rule our hearts,
may the word of Christ dwell in us richly;
whatever we do in word or deed
may we do all in the name of the Lord Jesus:
and the blessing of God almighty,
the Father, the Son and the Holy Spirit,
be with us always. **Amen.**

490 BLESSING
God's word, conference, witness, music
from Colossians 3

The word of Christ dwell in you richly
as you teach and counsel one another
    with all wisdom,
and as you sing psalms, hymns
    and spiritual songs
with gratitude in your hearts to God;
whatever you do in word or deed,
do all in the name of the Lord Jesus,
giving thanks to God the Father through him:
and the blessing of God almighty,
Father, Son and Holy Spirit,
be with you always. **Amen.**

491 BLESSING
God's word, conference, witness
from Colossians 3 (alternative)

May the word of Christ dwell in us richly
as we teach his wisdom and counsel one another,
as we sing psalms, hymns and spiritual songs
with heartfelt thanksgiving to God;
whatever we do in word or deed,
let us do all in the name of the Lord Jesus,
giving thanks to God the Father through him:
and the blessing of God almighty,
Father, Son and Holy Spirit,
be with us always. **Amen.**

492 BLESSING
Engagement, marriage, rededication
from 1 Thessalonians 3

God himself, our Father,
and our Lord Jesus Christ
direct *your* way together;
the Lord make *your* love for each other
increase and overflow;
the Lord strengthen *your* hearts
so that *you* will be blameless and holy
   in the presence of our God and Father
at the coming of our Lord Jesus Christ. **Amen.**

493 BLESSING
Renewal, witness, fellowship
from 1 Thessalonians 3 (variant)

The Lord make *your* love increase and overflow
for each other and for everyone else;
the Lord strengthen *your* hearts
so that *you* will be blameless and holy
   in the presence of our God and Father;
and the blessing of God almighty,
the Father, the Son and the Holy Spirit,
remain with *you* always. **Amen.**

494 BLESSING

Mission, ministry, service, commissioning
from 1 Thessalonians 5

Go in peace,
be very courageous,
hold on to what is good,
do not return evil for evil,
strengthen the faint-hearted,
support the weak,
help the afflicted,
honour all people,
love and serve the Lord,
rejoicing in the power of
    the Holy Spirit;
and the grace of the Lord Jesus
    be with you always. **Amen.**

495 BLESSING

Mission, ministry, service, commissioning
from 1 Thessalonians 5 (alternative)

Let us go out in peace
    and be very courageous,
holding on to what is good,
not returning evil for evil,
strengthening the faint-hearted,
supporting the weak,
helping the afflicted,
honouring all people,
loving and serving the Lord,
rejoicing in the power of
    the Holy Spirit;
and the grace of the Lord Jesus
    be with us always. **Amen.**

496 BLESSING
Advent, holiness
from 1 Thessalonians 5

God who gives us peace
make *you* holy in every way,
and keep *your* whole being –
   spirit, soul and body –
free from every fault
at the coming of our Lord Jesus Christ;
and the blessing of God
who is faithful,
Father, Son and Holy Spirit,
be with *you* always. **Amen.**

497 BLESSING
Baptism, confirmation, general
from 2 Thessalonians 2

The Lord Jesus Christ,
who loved *you*,
and by his grace gave *you*
eternal encouragement and good hope.
confirm *your* hearts,
and strengthen *you* in every good deed and word;
and the blessing of God almighty,
Father, Son and Holy Spirit,
be with *you* always. **Amen.**

498 BLESSING
Baptism, confirmation, pentecost
from 2 Thessalonians 2 and 3

God our Father,
who loved *you*,
and by his grace gave *you*
   eternal courage and good hope,
confirm *your* hearts, and strengthen *you*
in every good deed and word;
the Spirit of peace
give *you* peace at all times
   and in every way;
and the grace of our Lord Jesus Christ
   be with *you* all. **Amen.**

499 BLESSING
Baptism, confirmation, temptation
from 2 Thessalonians 3

The Lord, who is faithful,
strengthen you,
protect *you* from the evil one,
and lead *your* hearts in the love of God
and the endurance of Jesus Christ our Lord. **Amen.**

500 BLESSING
Renewal, general
from 2 Thessalonians 3

The Lord lead *your* hearts
into the love of God
and the patience of Christ:
and the blessing of God almighty,
the Father, the Son and the Holy Spirit,
be among *you* and remain with *you* always. **Amen.**

501 BLESSING
Peace, serenity, general
from 2 Thessalonians 3

The Lord of peace himself give *you* peace
at all times and in every way;
and the blessing of God almighty,
the Father, the Son and the Holy Spirit,
be with *you* always. **Amen.**

502 BLESSING
All Saints, discipleship
from 1 Timothy 6

Strive for righteousness, godlinesss, faith,
   love, endurance and gentleness;
run the race of faith,
take hold of eternal life
to which God called you
   when you confessed his name before the world;
and the blessing of God almighty,
the Father, the Son and the Holy Spirit,
be with you always. **Amen.**

503 BLESSING
All Saints, discipleship
from 1 Timothy 6 (alternative)

Let us strive for righteousness, godliness, faith,
   love, endurance and gentleness;
running the race of faith,
taking hold of eternal life
to which God called us
   when we confessed his name before the world;
and the blessing of God almighty,
the Father, the Son and the Holy Spirit,
be with us always. **Amen.**

504 BLESSING
Confirmation, discipleship
from 2 Timothy 1

Hold firmly
to the truths you have been taught
as the example for you to follow,
and remain in the faith and love
that are yours in Christ Jesus,
through the power of the Holy Spirit
   who lives in us.
And the blessing of God almighty,
the Father, the Son and the Holy Spirit,
be with you always. **Amen.**

505 BLESSING
Confirmation, discipleship
from 2 Timothy 1 (alternative)

Let us hold firm
to the truths we have been taught
as the example for us to follow,
remaining in the faith and love
that are ours in Christ Jesus,
through the power of the Holy Spirit
   who lives in us.
And the blessing of God almighty,
the Father, the Son and the Holy Spirit,
be with us always. **Amen.**

506 BLESSING
Witness, baptism, confirmation,
* commissioning*
from 2 Timothy 2

Be strong
through the grace that is yours
    in union with Christ Jesus;
take your part in suffering
    as his loyal soldier:
and the blessing of God almighty,
the Father, the Son and the Holy Spirit,
be with you always. **Amen.**

507 BLESSING
Witness, baptism, confirmation,
* commissioning*
from 2 Timothy 2 (alternative)

Let us be strong
through the grace that is ours
    in union with Christ Jesus,
taking our part in suffering
    as his loyal soldiers:
and the blessing of God almighty,
the Father, the Son and the Holy Spirit,
be with us always. **Amen.**

508 BLESSING
Advent, witness, ministry
from 2 Timothy 4

In the presence of God,
   and of Christ Jesus
who will judge the living and the dead,
and because he is coming as king:
preach the word,
be prepared at all times
whether people will listen or not;
always keep control of yourself,
endure suffering,
share the good news of Christ,
do the task that God has given you:
and the blessing of God almighty,
the Father, the Son and the Holy Spirit,
be with you always. **Amen.**

509 BLESSING
Advent, witness, ministry
from 2 Timothy 4 (alternative)

As servants of God, and of Christ Jesus
who will judge the living and the dead,
and because he is coming as king:
let us preach the word,
always prepared to speak
whether people will listen or not;
keeping control of ourselves,
enduring suffering,
sharing the good news of Christ,
doing the tasks that God has given us:
and the blessing of God almighty,
the Father, the Son and the Holy Spirit,
be with us always. **Amen.**

510 BLESSING
All Saints, farewell, commissioning
from 2 Timothy 4

Run the good race to the end,
keep the faith;
that you may receive
   the crown of righteousness,
which God the righteous judge
will give on that day
to those who have loved him
and long to see him:
and the blessing of God almighty,
Father, Son and Holy Spirit,
be with you always. **Amen.**

511 BLESSING
All Saints, farewell, commissioning
from 2 Timothy 4 (alternative)

Let us run the good race to the end,
let us keep the faith;
that we may receive
   the crown of righteousness,
which God the righteous judge
will give on that day
to those who have loved him
and long to see him:
and the blessing of God almighty,
Father, Son and Holy Spirit,
be with us always. **Amen.**

512 BLESSING
Passiontide, Pentecost, holiness, dedication
from Hebrews 9

By the blood of Christ,
through the eternal Spirit,
offer yourselves in holiness to God;
and the blessing of the Father,
    the Son and the Spirit
be with you always. **Amen.**

513 BLESSING
Passiontide, Pentecost, holiness, dedication
from Hebrews 9 (alternative)

By the blood of Christ,
through the eternal Spirit,
let us offer ourselves in holiness to God;
and the blessing of the Father,
    the Son and the Spirit
be with us always. **Amen.**

514 BLESSING
Passiontide, Ascensiontide, All Saints,
    discipleship, endurance
from Hebrews 12

Fix your eyes on Jesus,
the source and the fulfilment of our faith,
who for the joy set before him
endured the cross, scorning its shame,
and sat down at the right hand
    of the throne of God.
And the blessing of God almighty,
Father, Son and Holy Spirit,
be with you always. **Amen.**

515 BLESSING

Passiontide, Ascensiontide, All Saints,
*   discipleship, endurance*
from Hebrews 12 (alternative)

Let us fix our eyes on Jesus,
the source and the fulfilment of our faith,
who for the joy set before him
endured the cross, scorning its shame,
and sat down at the right hand
    of the throne of God.
And the blessing of God almighty,
Father, Son and Holy Spirit,
be with us always. **Amen.**

516 BLESSING

Easter, God as Shepherd, covenant,
*   commissioning*
from Hebrews 13

The God of peace,
who through the blood of the eternal covenant
brought back from the dead our Lord Jesus,
that great shepherd of the sheep,
equip *you* with every good gift
to do his will
[and to work in *you*
what is pleasing in his sight];
through Jesus Christ,
to whom be glory for ever and ever. **Amen.**

517 BLESSING
Lent, prayer, dependence on God
from 1 Peter 5

Humble yourselves under the mighty hand of God,
that in due time he may exalt you.
Cast all your anxieties upon him,
because he cares about you;
and the blessing of God almighty,
the Father, the Son and the Holy Spirit,
be with you always. **Amen.**

518 BLESSING
Lent, prayer, dependence on God
from 1 Peter 5 (alternative)

Let us humble ourselves under the mighty hand of God,
that in due time he might exalt us;
casting all our anxieties on him,
because he cares about us:
and the blessing of God almighty,
the Father, the Son and the Holy Spirit,
be with us always. **Amen.**

519 BLESSING
Heaven, calling, ministry, maturity
from 1 Peter 5

The God of all grace
who called *you* to his eternal glory in Christ,
make *you* strong, firm and steadfast:
to him be the power for ever and ever. Amen.

520 BLESSING
Heaven, calling, ministry, maturity
from 1 Peter 5 (variant)

The God of all grace
who called *you* to his eternal glory in Christ,
make *you* strong, firm and steadfast;
and the blessing of God the Father,
   the Son and the Spirit
be *yours* for ever. **Amen.**

521 BLESSING
Lent, discipleship, maturity
from 2 Peter 3

[*Let us*] Grow in the grace and knowledge
of our Lord and saviour Jesus Christ,
to whom be eternal glory;
and the blessing of God almighty,
the Father, the Son and the Holy Spirit,
be with *you* always. **Amen.**

522 BLESSING
Testing, endurance, God's word
from 1 John 2

Be strong,
let the word of God live in you
and so defeat the evil one;
and the blessing of God almighty,
the Father, the Son and the Holy Spirit
be with you always. **Amen.**

523 BLESSING
Advent, renewal, prayer, holiness
from 1 John 2

Remain one with Christ,
so that when he comes
you may be confident
and need not hide in shame:
and the blessing of God almighty,
the Father, the Son,
and the Spirit,
   be poured out upon you,
and remain with you always. **Amen.**

524 BLESSING
General
from 2 John

God the Father
and Jesus Christ, the Father's Son,
give *you* grace, mercy and peace;
may they be *yours* in truth and love for ever. **Amen.**

525 BLESSING
Discipleship, renewal, prayer, dying
from Jude

Build yourselves up
in your most holy faith,
pray in the Holy Spirit,
keep yourselves in the love of God,
and wait for the mercy
   of our Lord Jesus Christ
to bring you to eternal life.
And the blessing of God almighty,
the Father, the Son and the Holy Spirit,
be with you always. **Amen.**

526 BLESSING
Discipleship, renewal, prayer, dying
from Jude (alternative)

Let us build ourselves up
in our most holy faith,
pray in the Holy Spirit,
keep ourselves in the love of God,
and wait for the mercy
   of our Lord Jesus Christ
to bring us to eternal life.
And the blessing of God almighty,
the Father, the Son and the Holy Spirit,
be with us always. **Amen.**

527 BLESSING
Lent, temptation, All Saints
from Jude

Now to him who is able to keep *you* from falling,
and to present *you* faultless
   before the presence of his glory,
with exceeding joy,
to the only wise God, our Saviour,
be glory and majesty,
dominion and power;
and the blessing
of Father, Son and Holy Spirit,
be upon *you* now and for ever. **Amen.**

DISMISSAL

528 DISMISSAL
All Saints, testing
from Exodus 14

Do not be afraid,
stand your ground,
see the Lord's salvation;
and may God almighty go with you. **Amen.**

529 DISMISSAL
Evening
from Exodus 33

The presence of the Lord go with you;
the Lord give you rest. Amen.

530 DISMISSAL
Evening
from Exodus 33 (alternative)

The presence of the Lord go with *you*:
the Lord give us rest. Amen.

531 DISMISSAL
People of God, forgiveness, protection
from Exodus 33

Lord God almighty,
you have revealed your goodness to us
and proclaimed your name among us:
show us your glory.

You have mercy on us, and compassion;
in Christ you forgive our sins –
hide us in the cleft of the Rock:
cover us with your hand.

Lord, you know us by name;
in Christ we have found favour in your sight:
now let your presence go with us,
and give us rest. Amen.

532 DISMISSAL
Ascension, commissioning, ministry
from John 20

Jesus said,
'As the Father has sent me, I am sending you:
receive the Holy Spirit'.
Go in the name of Christ. **Amen.**

533 DISMISSAL
General
from 1 Corinthians 16

Let all who love the Lord be blessed:
come, O Lord.

Love to all of you in Christ Jesus:
the grace of the Lord Jesus be with you. Amen.

534 DISMISSAL
Advent, church, people of God
from Revelation 22

Jesus says, 'Behold I am coming soon!'
The Spirit and the bride say, 'Come!':
All who hear say, 'Come!'

Jesus, the faithful witness says,
'Yes, I am coming soon.'
Amen. Come, Lord Jesus.

The grace of the Lord Jesus
be with all God's people. **Amen.**

INDEX

SEASON AND SUBJECT INDEX

*indicates a 'personal' prayer – couched in individual terms.
Numbers refer to prayer items

Advent

Greeting: Grace and peace to you from him who is (Revelation 1.4) – 29
Approach: Lord, we come to you, Alpha and Omega (Matthew 24.3–14, 32–35) – 57
Approach: Come to worship the Lord – to Mount Zion (Hebrews 12.22–25) – 60
Commandments – prayer: You shall have no other gods but me (Exodus 20.3–17, Deuteronomy 5.7–21) – 62
Commandments – declaration: Lord, we will have no other God but you (Exodus 20.3–17, Deuteronomy 5.7–21) – 63
Commandments – before: Let us hear the decrees and the laws (Deuteronomy 5.1) – 64
Commandments – after: You have declared this day (Deuteronomy 26.17–18) – 65
Commandments – declaration: Our Lord God, you are the only Lord (Mark 12.29–31) – 67
Commandments – prayer: The commandments – do not commit adultery (Romans 13.9) – 68
Absolution: Hear God's tender words of comfort (Isaiah 40.1–5) – 139
Absolution: Hear God's tender words of comfort (Isaiah 40.1–5) – 140
Before Reading: You are our lamp, O Lord (2 Samuel 22.29) – 196
Creed: We believe in the Gospel, promised by God (Romans 1.2–4) – 206
Creed: We believe in God almighty (Revelation 1.5–8) – 230
Creed: We believe in God the Father, who created (Revelation 4.11, 5.9, 22.20) – 232
For ourselves – Advent: When the skies grow dark and buildings fall (Mark 13.2–27) – 313
Acclamation: O Lord, we exalt and praise your name (Isaiah 25.1–9) – 373
Doxology: Lord almighty, you bring low all pride (Isaiah 23.9–11, 24.6–16) – 379
Blessing: Strengthen the feeble hands (Isaiah 35.2–4) – 435
Blessing: God who gives us peace (1 Thessalonians 5.23–24) – 496
Blessing: In the presence of God, (2 Timothy 4.1–2) – 508
Blessing: As servants of God, and of Christ Jesus (2 Timothy 4.1–2) – 509
Blessing: Remain one with Christ, (1 John 2.28) – 523
Dismissal: Jesus says, 'Behold I am coming soon!' (Revelation 22.17–21) – 534

All Saints

Greeting: Grace to all who love our Lord Jesus Christ (Ephesians 6.18) – 13
Greeting: Grace and peace to you from God who is (Revelation 1.4–5) – 30
Greeting: Grace and peace to you from Jesus Christ (Revelation 1.4–5) – 31
Approach: Come to worship the Lord – to Mount Zion (Hebrews 12.22–25) – 60
Absolution: God has rescued you from the power of darkness (Colossians 1.13–14) – 158
Creed: We believe in God almighty (Revelation 1.5–8) – 230
Thanksgiving: O Lord God, we acknowledge your strength (Psalm 29.1–11) – 338

Thanksgiving: Hear the promises of Jesus (Revelation 2.7–26, 3.4–5) – 367
Doxology/Ascription: Now to him who is able to keep us (Jude 1.24) – 395
Blessing: Strengthen the feeble hands (Isaiah 35.2–4) – 435
Blessing: Be on your guard (1 Corinthians 16.13) – 455
Blessing: Let us be on our guard (1 Corinthians 16.13) – 456
Blessing: God, from the wealth of his glory (Ephesians 3.16–19) – 474
Blessing: Strive for righteousness, godliness, faith (1 Timothy 6.11–12) – 502
Blessing: Let us strive for righteousness, godliness (1 Timothy 6.11–12) – 503
Blessing: Run the good race to the end (2 Timothy 4.7–8) – 510
Blessing: Let us run the good race to the end (2 Timothy 4.7–8) – 511
Blessing: Fix your eyes on Jesus (Hebrews 12.2) – 514
Blessing: Let us fix our eyes on Jesus (Hebrews 12.2) – 515
Blessing: Now to him who is able to keep you (Jude 1.24–25) – 527
Dismissal: Do not be afraid, stand your ground (Exodus 14.13) – 528

ambition

Blessing: Set your heart on things above (Colossians 3.1) – 484
Blessing: Let us set our hearts on things above (Colossians 3.1) – 485

anniversary

Approach: O Lord our God, there is no God like you (1 Kings 8.22–30) – 34
Exhortation: Sing praise to the Lord, all his faithful people (Psalm 30.4) – 164
Blessing: The Lord, the maker of heaven and earth (Psalm 134.1–3) – 433

anxiety

Absolution: The Lord knows your voice (Psalm 116.1–7) – 123
Absolution: The Lord knows our voice (Psalm 116.1–7) – 124

Ascension

Approach: Lord, you are king, and we tremble before you (Psalm 99.1–9) – 45
Exhortation: Let us sing to the Lord our God (Exodus 15.1–21) – 163
Exhortation: Come, let us bow down in worship (Psalm 95.6) – 170
Exhortation: Sing a new song to the Lord (Psalm 96.1–2) – 171
Exhortation: The Lord, our mighty God, is king (Revelation 19.6–7) – 191
Exhortation: The Lord, our mighty God, is king (Revelation 19.6–7) – 192
Exhortation: Praise God – The Lord our almighty God is king (Revelation 19.6–7) – 193
Creed: We believe God raised from the dead (Ephesians 1.20–23) – 215
Creed: Jesus Christ, the Son of God (Philippians 2.5–11) – 218
Creed: Let us proclaim the mystery of our faith (1 Timothy 3.16) – 222
Thanksgiving: We praise you, our God, because you have (Philippians 2.9–11)   364
Acclamation: Who is like you, Lord our God (Exodus 15.11–21) – 368
Doxology/Ascription: To our Lord and saviour Jesus Christ (2 Peter 3.18) – 394
Blessing: Set your heart on things above (Colossians 3.1) – 484
Blessing: Let us set our hearts on things above (Colossians 3.1) – 485
Blessing: Fix your eyes on Jesus (Hebrews 12.2) – 514
Blessing: Let us fix our eyes on Jesus (Hebrews 12.2) – 515
Dismissal: Jesus said, 'As the Father has sent me..' (John 20.21–22) – 532

assurance

Greeting: You are loved by God the Father (Jude 1.1–2) – 28
Absolution: In the time of his favour (Isaiah 49.8–26) – 146
Absolution: In the time of salvation (Isaiah 49.8–26) – 147
Absolution: You who once were far away (Ephesians 2.13–14) – 157
For ourselves – assurance: Living God, give us faith to be sure (Hebrews 11.1–39) – 328

atonement

Creed: We believe Christ died for sins once for all (1 Peter 3.18–22) – 227

authority of Christ

    Creed: We believe in Jesus Christ (Revelation 1.17–18) – 231

awareness

    Blessing: Forgive each other (Colossians 3.13–14) – 486
    Blessing: Let us forgive each other (Colossians 3.13–14) – 487

baptism

    Creed: We have been crucified with Christ (Galatians 2.19–20) – 214
    Creed: We believe in one body, the church (Ephesians 4.) – 217
    Creed: We believe in God who saved us (Titus 3.4–8) – 224
    Dedication – presentation of a Bible: The words of this book (Deuteronomy 6.6–7) – 233
    Dedication – a child: Almighty God, we bring our child (1 Samuel 1.25–28) – 234
    Declaration: Do you know into what (Romans 6.1–11) – 238
    For ourselves – dedication/Easter/Baptism: Our Saviour Jesus Christ (Romans 14.7–9) – 316
    Blessing: The spirit of the Lord rest upon you (Isaiah 11.2–3) – 434
    Blessing: Christ our saviour, the Lord of the living (Romans 14.7–9) – 450
    Blessing: The Lord Jesus Christ, who loved you (2 Thessalonians 2.16–17) – 497
    Blessing: God our Father, who loved you (2 Thessalonians 2.16–17, 3.16) – 498
    Blessing: The Lord, who is faithful (2 Thessalonians 3.3–5) – 499
    Blessing: Be strong through the grace that is yours (2 Timothy 2.1–4) – 506
    Blessing: Let us be strong through the grace (2 Timothy 2.1–4) – 507

behaviour

    For ourselves – right behaviour: Lord, hear us when we call to you (Psalm 141.1–10) – 297
    For ourselves – right behaviour: Lord, hear me when I call to you* (Psalm 141.1–10) – 298
    For ourselves – right behaviour: Lord, we call to you (Psalm 141.1–10) – 299

blessing *See also numbers 402–527.*

    For ourselves – God's blessing: Lord God, lead us in the way of holiness (Isaiah 35.8–10) – 307

calling

    Doxology/Ascription: To the God of all grace who called us (1 Peter 5.11) – 393
    Blessing: The God of all grace (1 Peter 5.10–11) – 519
    Blessing: The God of all grace (1 Peter 5.10–11) – 520

celebration *See also 'worship'.*

    Exhortation: Sing praise to the Lord, all his faithful (Psalm 30.4) – 164
    Exhortation: Shout for joy to the Lord, all the earth (Psalm 100.1–4) – 175
    Thanksgiving: O Lord God, you are great and most worthy (Psalm 48.1–14) – 344
    Thanksgiving: Lord God, you are King of the earth (Psalm 97.1–12) – 347
    Acclamation: O Lord, we exalt and praise your name (Isaiah 25.1–9) – 373

children *See 'family', 'parents'.*

    For others – our children: Lord, let us not keep from our children (Psalm 78.4–7) – 243

choir *See also 'music'.*

    Exhortation: All of you who serve the Lord (Psalm 134.1–3) – 184

Christ-likeness

    For ourselves – Christ-likeness: God of grace, we have no righteousness (Philippians 3.8–11) – 321

Christmas

    Absolution: Hear God's tender words of comfort (Isaiah 40.1–5) – 139
    Absolution: Hear God's tender words of comfort (Isaiah 40.1–5) – 140
    Creed: Let us declare our faith in the Son of God (John 1.1–14) – 204
    Creed: We believe in the Gospel, promised by God (Romans 1.2–4) – 206

Creed: We believe in Christ, the image of God (Colossians 1.15–18) – 220
Creed: We believe in God who has spoken to us (Hebrews 1.2–3) – 225
Thanksgiving: We bless you, our Lord God (Luke 1.68–79) – 357

church *See 'people of God'.*
   Approach: Come to worship the Lord – to Mount Zion (Hebrews 12.22–25) – 60
   Creed: We believe God raised from the dead (Ephesians 1.20–23) – 215
   Creed: We believe in Christ, the image of God (Colossians 1.15–20) – 219
   Creed: We believe in Christ, the image of God (Colossians 1.15–18) – 220
   Creed: We believe in God almighty (Revelation 1.5–8) – 230
   Doxology/Ascription: To him who loves us (Revelation 1.5–6) – 396
   Doxology: You are worthy, Lord our God (Revelation 4.11, 5.9–13) – 398
   Blessing: Remain in Jesus Christ (John 15.4–12) – 446
   Blessing: Let us remain in Jesus Christ (John 15.4–12) – 447
   Dismissal: Jesus says, 'Behold I am coming soon!' (Revelation 22.17–21) – 534

church anniversary
   Approach: O Lord our God, there is no God like you (1 Kings 8.22–30) – 34
   Approach: Lord, thank you for this building (Psalm 26.5–8) – 39
   Exhortation: Praise God in his sanctuary (Psalm 150.1–6) – 186
   After Reading: If you have a mind to hear (Revelation 1 – 7) – 199
   Response: Hear what the Spirit is saying (Revelation 1 – 7) – 200
   Thanksgiving: Lord God of our fathers (1 Chronicles 29.10–13) – 331
   Thanksgiving: Lord God, we thank you that in Christ (Psalm 26.3–8) – 337
   Thanksgiving: O Lord God, we acknowledge your strength (Psalm 29.1–11) – 338
   Thanksgiving: O Lord God, you are great and most worthy (Psalm 48.1–14) – 344
   Acclamation: Lord God, may you be praised for ever (1 Chronicles 29.10–13) – 370
   Acclamation: Yours, Lord, is the greatness (1 Chronicles 29.10–13) – 371
   Doxology: O Lord, holy One, with all the hosts (Psalm 29.1–11) – 377
   Doxology: Lord God, our God, we have seen you (Psalm 63.2–5) – 378
   Doxology/Ascription: Now to God the Father who is able to do (Ephesians 3.20–21) – 386
   Blessing: The Lord, the maker of heaven and earth (Psalm 134.1–3) – 433

civic
   Greeting: Grace and peace to you (Romans 1.7) – 3
   Greeting: The God of peace be with you all (Romans 15.33) – 5
   Greeting: Grace and peace from God the Father (Titus 1.4) – 19
   Confession: Lord God, we are not worthy (Psalm 15.1–5) – 74
   Confession: Lord our God, we confess (Isaiah 43.22–25) – 87
   Confession: Lord God, our offences are many in your sight (Isaiah 59.12–13) – 89
   Doxology/Ascription: To God, the blessed and only Ruler (1 Timothy 6.15–16) – 389
   Blessing: The blessing of the Lord be upon you (Psalm 129.8) – 432

cleansing *See also 'forgiveness'.*
   Approach: Lord of the earth and everything in it (Psalm 24.1–6) – 38
   For ourselves – cleansing: Lord God, our refuge and our redeemer (Psalm 19.12–14) – 267

comfort
   Absolution: The faithful Lord, the sovereign Lord (Isaiah 25.8–9) – 136
   Absolution: The faithful Lord, the sovereign Lord (Isaiah 25.8–9) – 137

commandments *See numbers 62–68.*
   Confession: Lord, we have not obeyed your word (2 Kings 22.13–20) – 70
   Confession: Our Lord God, great, mighty and awesome (Nehemiah 9.32–37) – 72
   Confession: O Lord our God, we have not obeyed (Psalm 106.6–47) – 80
   Confession: Lord, we are to blame (Psalm 119.1–8) – 82
   For ourselves – God's laws: Lord, you have given us your laws (Psalm 119.4–7) – 282

Approach: Almighty Lord, all the earth shouts joy (Psalm 100.1–5) – 46
Approach: O God, we have come to worship you (Psalm 148.1–14) – 54
Approach: See, the winter is past (Song of Songs 2.11–13) – 56
Absolution: God who is merciful and loving (Psalm 103.8–12) – 119
Absolution: The Lord, whose love for those who seek him (Psalm 103.11–13) – 122
Exhortation: Shout with joy to God, all the earth (Psalm 66.1–8) – 166
Creed: We believe in one God who made all things (Isaiah 44.2–24) – 203
Creed: We believe in God who has spoken to us (Hebrews 1.2–3) – 225
Thanksgiving: O Lord our Lord, we thank you that your name (Psalm 8.1–7) – 332
Thanksgiving: God our Father, we thank you (Psalm 136.1–24) – 351
Acclamation: Blessed be your glorious name, O Lord our God (Nehemiah 9.5–6) – 372
Doxology: O Lord, holy One, with all the hosts (Psalm 29.1–11) – 377
Blessing: God who made the heavens (Psalm 8.3–9) – 412
Blessing: God, whose glory the heavens declare (Psalm 19.1–8) – 413
Blessing: God, whose invisible qualities (Romans 1.17–20) – 449

death
For others – the dying: Lord, now let your servant depart (Luke 2.29–32) – 250

dedication *See also numbers 233–239.*
Approach: O Lord our God, there is no God like you (1 Kings 8.22–30) – 34
Approach: Lord, thank you for this building (Psalm 26.5–8) – 39
Exhortation: Praise the Lord, you servants of the Lord (Psalm 113.1) – 183
Exhortation: Praise God in his sanctuary (Psalm 150.1–6) – 186
After Reading: If you have a mind to hear (Revelation 1 – 7) – 199
Response: Hear what the Spirit is saying (Revelation 1.) – 200
Creed: We have been crucified with Christ (Galatians 2.19–20) – 214
Dedication – Presentation of a Bible: The words of this book (Deuteronomy 6.6–7) – 233
Dedication – a child: Almighty God, we bring our child (1 Samuel 1.25–28) – 234
For ourselves – dedication/Easter/Baptism: Our Saviour Jesus Christ (Romans 14.7–9) – 316
Thanksgiving: Lord God of our fathers (1 Chronicles 29.10–13) – 331
Thanksgiving: Lord God, we thank you that in Christ (Psalm 26.3–8) – 337
Thanksgiving: O Lord God, we acknowledge your strength (Psalm 29.1–11) – 338
Thanksgiving: Lord God, you heard my cry* (Psalm 40.1–10) – 343
Thanksgiving: O Lord God, you are great and most worthy (Psalm 48.1–14) – 344
Acclamation: Lord God, may you be praised for ever (1 Chronicles 29.10–13) – 370
Acclamation: Yours, Lord, is the greatness (1 Chronicles 29.10–13) – 371
Doxology: Glory be to you, our God (Revelation 15.3) – 400
Doxology: Glory be to you, our God (Revelation 15.3) – 401
Blessing: The Lord answer you when you are in distress (Psalm 20.1–5) – 414
Blessing: By the blood of Christ (Hebrews 9.14) – 512
Blessing: By the blood of Christ (Hebrews 9.14) – 513

deliverance
Approach: O God, we love you (Psalm 18.1–17, 49–50) – 37
For ourselves – deliverance: O Lord, we trust in you (Psalm 31.14–16) – 275
For ourselves – deliverance: O Lord, we wait for you in hope (Psalm 33.20–22) – 276
Thanksgiving: God our Father, we thank you (Psalm 136.1–24) – 351
Doxology/Ascription: To the Lord who rescues us from every evil (2 Timothy 4.18) – 391

dependence on God *See also 'faith'.*
Approach: We praise you, O Lord, for you hear our cry (Psalm 28.6–9) – 41
Thanksgiving: God, my protector, I trust you for my safety* (Psalm 16.1–8) – 334
Blessing: Humble yourselves under the mighty hand (1 Peter 5.6–7) – 517
Blessing: Let us humble ourselves (1 Peter 5.6–7) – 518

expectancy
Approach: Lord of the earth and everything in it (Psalm 24.1–6) – 38
Approach: O God, we have come to your house (Ecclesiastes 5.1–7) – 55

faith *See also numbers 201–232.*
Confession: God our Father, you have given your divine (Acts 3.13–19) – 98
Absolution: The Lord God have mercy on you (Psalm 51.1–10) – 111
Absolution: The Lord has mercy on you (Psalm 51.1–10) – 112
Absolution: The Lord, your redeemer, the Holy One (Isaiah 43.25) – 143
Absolution: The Lord, your redeemer, the Holy One (Isaiah 43.25) – 144
Absolution: This is what the Lord says (Isaiah 43.25) – 145
Absolution: God has rescued you from the power of darkness (Colossians 1.13–14) – 158
Absolution: Draw near with a sincere heart (Hebrews 10.22–23) – 159
Absolution: Let us draw near with a sincere heart (Hebrews 10.22–23) – 160
Exhortation: The Lord has redeemed us (Psalm 107.20–21) – 180
Creed: We believe in the Lord God, the Holy One (Isaiah 43.10–25) – 202
Creed: We believe in the Gospel, promised by God (Romans 1.2–4) – 206
Creed: Jesus is Lord; God has raised him (Romans 10.8–10) – 207
For ourselves – faith: O God, who because of our faith (Romans 4.16) – 315
Thanksgiving: God our Father, we thank you (Psalm 118.1–14) – 350
Thanksgiving: We praise you, God and Father (Ephesians 1.3–7) – 363
Doxology/Ascription: Now to God the Father who is able to do (Ephesians 3.20–21) – 386
Blessing: Wait for the Lord in hope (Psalm 33.20–22) – 417
Blessing: Let us wait for the Lord in hope (Psalm 33.20–22) – 418
Blessing: Wait for the Lord in hope (Psalm 33.20–22) – 419
Blessing: The God of hope fill you with all joy (Romans 15.13) – 453
Blessing: God, from the wealth of his glory (Ephesians 3.16–19) – 474

faithfulness of God
Creed: We believe in God, who is gracious (Psalm 145.13–16) – 201

family
Greeting: Peace to you . . . greet your friends by name (3 John 1.14) – 27
Approach: Lord, our God, this is the place (Deuteronomy 12.5–21) – 33
Approach: Lord, we rejoiced when we heard (Psalm 122.1–9) – 51
Approach: O God, we have come to worship you (Psalm 148.1–14) – 54
Creed: We believe in God the Father (Ephesians 3.14–17) – 216
For ourselves – home and work: Lord of our praise, strengthen us (Psalm 112.1–10) – 281
For ourselves – families: Lord, help us to build our homes (Psalm 127.1–5) – 294
Thanksgiving: God our Father, gracious and compassionate (Psalm 145.8–21) – 353
Thanksgiving: We thank you, God our Father (Isaiah 59.1–21) – 354
Blessing: The Lord bless you all the days of your life (Psalm 128.5–6) – 431

farewell
Blessing: Run the good race to the end (2 Timothy 4.7–8) – 510
Blessing: Let us run the good race to the end (2 Timothy 4.7–8) – 511

fellowship
For others – fellowship: God our Father, always when we pray (Romans 1.10–12) – 252
Blessing: Remain in Jesus Christ (John 15.4–12) – 446
Blessing: Let us remain in Jesus Christ (John 15.4–12) – 447
Blessing: The God of patience and encouragement (Romans 15.5–6) – 452
Blessing: The grace of the Lord Jesus Christ (2 Corinthians 13.14) – 472
Blessing: The Lord make your love increase and overflow (1 Thessalonians 3.12–13) – 493

flower festival
Doxology: Lord God, our God, we have seen you (Psalm 63.2–5) – 378

forgiveness *See also numbers 101–162.*
Absolution: Praise the Lord – although he was angry (Isaiah 12.1–2) – 134

Absolution: Praise the Lord – although he was angry (Isaiah 12.1–2) – 135
Exhortation: Praise the Lord and do not forget (Psalm 103.1–5) – 176
Creed: We believe in the Lord God, the Holy One (Isaiah 43.10–25) – 202
For ourselves – forgiveness: O Lord, I pray to you because I trust you* (Psalm 25.1–12) – 272
Thanksgiving: Lord, thank you that you are willing (Psalm 32.1–11) – 340
Thanksgiving: We praise you, God and Father (Ephesians 1.3–7) – 363
Blessing: God almighty, who has revealed his goodness (Exodus 33.19–22) – 402
Blessing: The Lord hear your prayer (Psalm 102.1–19) – 425
Blessing: The Lord guide you and restore his comfort (Isaiah 57.18–19) – 439
Blessing: The Lord look upon your need and heal you (Isaiah 57.18–19) – 440
Blessing: Forgive each other (Colossians 3.13–14) – 486
Blessing: Let us forgive each other (Colossians 3.13–14) – 487
Dismissal: Lord God almighty, you have revealed (Exodus 33.19–22) – 531

fruitfulness
For ourselves – fruitfulness: God, our guide and protector (Psalm 1.2–4) – 260

funeral
Blessing: Christ our saviour, the Lord of the living (Romans 14.7–9) – 450

gifts
Creed: We believe in the one Holy Spirit (1 Corinthians 12.4) – 210

giving
Thanksgiving: Lord God our Father, thank you for the riches (Romans 11.33–36) – 361
Acclamation: Lord God, may you be praised for ever (1 Chronicles 29.10–13) – 370
Acclamation: Yours, Lord, is the greatness (1 Chronicles 29.10–13) – 371

Good Friday *See 'Passiontide', 'redemption'.*
Absolution: Receive God's forgiveness (Isaiah 53.4–5) – 148
Absolution: Let us receive God's forgiveness (Isaiah 53.4–5) – 149
Creed: We believe in Christ, the image of God (Colossians 1.15–20) – 219
Thanksgiving: Jesus Christ, faithful witness, firstborn (Revelation 1.5–6) – 366
Doxology: You are worthy, O Lord our God (Revelation 4.11, 5.9–13) – 397

goodness
For ourselves – goodness: Lord God, our saviour, we trust in you (Psalm 25.2–21) – 273

guidance
Approach: O Lord, you have searched us and you know us (Psalm 139.1–12) – 53
For ourselves – guidance: God our protector – we trust in you (Psalm 16.1–11) – 265
For ourselves – guidance: Lord God, let us hear your voice (Psalm 143.8–10) – 304
Doxology/Ascription: To the God of all wisdom and knowledge (Romans 11.33–36) – 382
Blessing: God the Father fill you with the knowledge (Colossians 1.9–12) – 483

guilt *See also 'forgiveness'.*
Confession: O God, we are too ashamed and disgraced (Ezra 9.5–15) – 71
Absolution: Draw near with a sincere heart (Hebrews 10.22–23) – 159
Absolution: Let us draw near with a sincere heart (Hebrews 10.22–23) – 160

harmony
Blessing: Strive for perfection (2 Corinthians 13.11) – 468
Blessing: Let us strive for perfection (2 Corinthians 13.11) – 469
Blessing: Be of one mind, live in peace (2 Corinthians 13.11) – 470
Blessing: Let us be of one mind (2 Corinthians 13.11) – 471

Harvest
Greeting: The Lord be with you (Ruth 2.4) – 1
Approach: Almighty Lord, all the earth shouts joy (Psalm 100.1–5) – 46
Exhortation: Come, let us sing for joy to the Lord (Psalm 95.1–2) – 168

Exhortation: Come, let us sing for joy to the Lord (Psalm 95.1–2) – 169
Thanksgiving: Our God, we come to praise you together (Psalm 65.1–13) – 345
Thanksgiving: Living God, you made heaven and earth (Acts 14.15–17) – 360

healing
Approach: Lord, you are our light and our salvation (Psalm 27.1–13) – 40
Absolution: The Lord God be merciful to you and heal you (Psalm 6.2–4) – 103
Absolution: Because you have remembered the Lord your God (Jonah 2.2–9) – 153
Absolution: Because we have remembered the Lord our God (Jonah 2.2–9) – 154
Exhortation: Praise the Lord and do not forget (Psalm 103.1–5) – 176
For others – preachers and healers: Sovereign Lord, you made the heaven (Acts 4.24–30) – 251
For ourselves -healing: Lord, heal us and we shall be healed (Jeremiah 17.14) – 310
For ourselves – healing: Lord, heal me, and I will be healed* (Jeremiah 17.14) – 311
Thanksgiving: We thank you, Sovereign Lord (Acts 4.24–30) – 359
Blessing: Wait for the Lord in hope (Psalm 33.20–22) – 419
Blessing: The Lord your Shepherd tenderly care for you (Isaiah 40.11) – 438
Blessing: The Lord guide you and restore his comfort (Isaiah 57.18–19) – 439
Blessing: The Lord look upon your need and heal you (Isaiah 57.18–19) – 440

heaven
Approach: Praise be to you, our God (1 Peter 1.3–9) – 61
Confession: Lord, we need you; our hearts are wounded (Psalm 109.22–26) – 81
Creed: We speak because we believe (2 Corinthians 4.13–16, 5.7) – 213
Creed: We believe in God the Father who has revealed (Titus 2.14, 3.4–7) – 223
Creed: We believe in God who saved us (Titus 3.4–8) – 224
Creed: We believe in Jesus Christ (Revelation 1.17–18) – 231
Thanksgiving: We thank you, our God, the Father (1 Peter 1.3–6) – 365
Blessing: The God of all grace (1 Peter 5.10–11) – 519
Blessing: The God of all grace (1 Peter 5.10–11) – 520

holidays
Approach: We stand up and praise you, Lord our God (Nehemiah 9.5–6) – 35

holiness
Exhortation: Worship the Lord in the splendour (Psalm 96.9–4) – 172
Acclamation: Great and marvellous are your deeds (Revelation 15.3–4) – 375
Blessing: God who gives us peace (1 Thessalonians 5.23–24) – 496
Blessing: By the blood of Christ (Hebrews 9.14) – 512
Blessing: By the blood of Christ (Hebrews 9.14) – 513
Blessing: Remain one with Christ (1 John 2.28) – 523

holiness of God
Absolution: The Lord our God answers your prayer (Psalm 99.8–9) – 115
Absolution: May the Lord our God answer our prayers (Psalm 99.8–9) – 116

Holy Communion
Greeting: Grace to all who love our Lord Jesus Christ (Ephesians 6.18) – 13
Greeting: Peace to all of you who are in Christ (1 Peter 5.14) – 24
Greeting: Peace to you . . . greet your friends by name (3 John 1.14) – 27
Approach: Lord, thank you for this building (Psalm 26.5–8) – 39
Approach: O God, you are our God and we long for you (Psalm 63.1–8) – 42
Approach: O Lord, we thank you for your greatness (Psalm 105.1–8) – 47
Approach: Lord Jesus Christ, we are your disciples (Luke 24.29–34) – 59
Approach: Come to worship the Lord – to Mount Zion (Hebrews 12.22–25) – 60
Commandments – confession: Jesus said – Love the Lord your God (Mark 12.29–31) – 66
Commandments – prayer: The commandments – do not commit adultery (Romans 13.9) – 68
Absolution: Because God loves you (1 John 4.10) – 162

Exhortation: Sing praise to the Lord, all his faithful (Psalm 30.4) – 164
Creed: We believe in one God and Father (1 Corinthians 8.6, 12.13) – 208
Declaration: What does this ceremony mean? (Exodus 13.14, Matthew 26.26–29, Mark 14.24, Luke 22.20, 1 Corinthians 11.23–26) – 239
Thanksgiving: O Lord, you are our Lord (Psalm 16.2–9) – 335
Thanksgiving: We thank you, our Father (Psalm 36.1–8) – 342
Thanksgiving: God our Father, we, the family of your people (Psalm 111.1–5) – 348
Thanksgiving: Heavenly Father, we thank you that when (1 Corinthians 11.23–26) – 356
Thanksgiving: Heavenly Father, we thank you that when (Luke 22.20) – 356
Thanksgiving: Heavenly Father, we thank you that when (Mark 14.24) – 356
Thanksgiving: Heavenly Father, we thank you that when (Matthew 26.26–29) – 356
Thanksgiving: Lord Jesus Christ, we are your disciples (Luke 24.29–34) – 358

Holy Spirit *See 'Pentecost', 'renewal'.*

hope *See 'Advent', 'salvation' and numbers 402–527.*
For ourselves – hope: Lord Jesus, you will come from heaven (1 Thessalonians 4.13–17) – 323

humility
For ourselves – humility: Lord God, keep our hearts from pride (Psalm 131.1–3) – 295
For ourselves – humility: Lord God, keep my heart from pride* (Psalm 131.1–3) – 296

illness *See also 'healing'.*
Thanksgiving: Lord God, I want to praise you* (Psalm 30.1–12) – 339

installation *See also 'commission'.*
Commendation – A Woman Minister: I commend to you our sister (Romans 16.1–2) – 236
Commendation – A Man Minister: I commend to you our brother (Philippians 2.29–30) – 237

invitation to faith *See also 'faith'.*
Greeting: Grace and peace be with you (1 John 1.8–9) – 10
Greeting: Grace and peace be yours in full measure (2 Peter 1.2) – 25
Confession: Lord, we cry to you (Psalm 130.1–5) – 83
Confession: God our Father, if we say that we have no sin (1 John 1.8) – 99
Confession: Lord God, you have taught us (1 John 1.8–9) – 100
Absolution: God in his goodness have mercy on you (Psalm 51.1–7) – 110
Absolution: God, the righteous judge (Psalm 51.1–12) – 113
Absolution: God who is merciful and loving (Psalm 103.8–12) – 119
Absolution: The Lord, whose love for those who seek him (Psalm 103.11–13) – 122
Absolution: The Lord restore you; the Lord bring you (Isaiah 38.16–17) – 138
After Reading: Those who have a mind to hear (Mark 4.9) – 198

joy *See also numbers 402–527.*
Blessing: The God of hope fill you with all joy (Romans 15.13) – 453

judgement
Doxology: Lord almighty, you bring low all pride (Isaiah 23.9–11, 24.14–16) – 379

justice
Approach: Lord, you are king, and we tremble before you (Psalm 99.1–9) – 45
Approach: O Lord, we thank you for your greatness (Psalm 105.1–8) – 47
Acclamation: Lord God almighty, what you have done (Revelation 15.3–4) – 376

leaders *See also 'commission', 'installation', 'ministry'.*
Approach: Lord almighty, how we love this place (Psalm 84.1–12) – 43

Lent
Greeting: Peace and mercy to the people of God (Galatians 6.16) – 11
Approach: Lord, we come to you, Alpha and Omega (Matthew 24.3–14, 32–35) – 57

Thanksgiving: O Lord God, we acknowledge your strength (Psalm 29.1–11) – 338
Doxology: Glory be to you, our God (Revelation 15.3) – 400
Doxology: Glory be to you, our God (Revelation 15.3) – 401

trouble

Confession: Lord, we have failed you – darkness overtakes us (Psalm 143.1–10) – 85
For others – In trouble: Be merciful, Lord, to all those in trouble (Psalm 31.9–12) – 242
For ourselves – In time of trouble: Lord God of heaven, you rule over states (2 Chronicles 20.6–12) – 258
For ourselves – In trouble: Be merciful, Lord, for I am in trouble* (Psalm 31.9–15) – 274
For ourselves – In trouble: Lord, when we pray, don't turn away from us (Psalm 55.1–22) – 279
Thanksgiving: O Lord God, we thank you that you reign (Psalm 9.7–10) – 333
Blessing: God is your strength and shield (Psalm 46.1–7) – 422
Blessing: Never be discouraged (2 Corinthians 4.16–18) – 462
Blessing: Let us never be discouraged (2 Corinthians 4.16–18) – 463

trust

Approach: Lord almighty, how we love this place (Psalm 84.1–12) – 43
For ourselves – Trust: Lord God, we remember days gone by (Psalm 143.5–8) – 303
Blessing: Trust the Lord and do right (Psalm 37.3–7) – 420
Blessing: Let us trust in the Lord and do right (Psalm 37.3–7) – 421
Blessing: Trust in the Lord (Isaiah 26.3–9) – 436
Blessing: Let us trust in the Lord (Isaiah 26.3–9) – 437

tyranny

For others – Tyranny and terrorism: Lord, you listen to the prayers of the lowly (Psalm 10.10–18) – 240

unity

Greeting: Welcome one another (Romans 15.7) – 4
Greeting: Peace and mercy to the people of God (Galatians 6.16) – 11
Greeting: Greetings, friends in the faith (Titus 3.15) – 21
Greeting: The grace of the Lord Jesus be with God's people (Revelation 22.21) – 32
Confession: Lord our God, you brought your people out (Daniel 9.15–20) – 95
Exhortation: Glorify the Lord with me (Psalm 34.3) – 165
Creed: We believe in one God and Father (1 Corinthians 8.6, 12.13) – 208
Creed: There is one God and Father (1 Corinthians 8.6, 12.13) – 209
Creed: We believe in one body, the church (Ephesians 4.) – 217
Thanksgiving: We thank you, our God, for our unity (1 Corinthians 12.4–6) – 362
Blessing: The God of strength and encouragement (Romans 15.5–6) – 451
Blessing: The God of patience and encouragement (Romans 15.5–6) – 452
Blessing: Strive for perfection (2 Corinthians 13.11) – 468
Blessing: Let us strive for perfection (2 Corinthians 13.11) – 469
Blessing: Be of one mind, live in peace (2 Corinthians 13.11) – 470
Blessing: Let us be of one mind (2 Corinthians 13.11) – 471
Blessing: Peace be to you and love with faith (Ephesians 6.23–24) – 477

visiting

Greeting: Greetings to the church of God (1 Corinthians 1.2–3) – 6
Greeting: Grace and peace to you (1 Thessalonians 1.1) – 16
Greeting: Greetings, friends in the faith (Titus 3.15) – 21
Blessing: Peace be to you and love with faith (Ephesians 6.23–24) – 477

walking with God See also 'prayer', 'presence of God'.
For ourselves – That we may walk in God's light: O God, you are light (1 John 1.5–7) – 330

weakness
For others – In weakness: Lord Jesus, the friend of all who obey you (Psalm 25.15–21) – 241

BIBLE REFERENCE INDEX

indicates a 'personal' prayer – couched in individual terms.

Exodus

5.7–21 Lord, we will have no other God but you (Commandments: Declaration) – 63
13.14 What does this ceremony mean? (Declaration) – 239
14.13 Do not be afraid, stand your ground (Dismissal) – 528
15.1–21 Let us sing to the Lord our God (Exhortation) – 163
15.11–21 Who is like you, Lord our God (Acclamation) – 368
20.3–17 You shall have no other gods but me (Commandments: Prayer) – 62
20.3–17 Lord, we will have no other God but you (Commandments: Declaration) – 63
33.14 The presence of the Lord go with you (Dismissal) – 529
33.19–22 God almighty, who has revealed his goodness (Blessing) – 402
33.19–22 Lord God almighty, you have revealed (Dismissal) – 531
34.6–9 Lord, the only God, compassionate (Confession) – 69

Numbers

6.24–26 The Lord bless you and keep you (Blessing) – 403
6.24–26 The Lord bless you and take care of you (Blessing) – 404
6.24–26 The Lord bless you and keep you (Blessing) – 405
6.24–26 The Lord bless you and watch over you (Blessing) – 406

Deuteronomy

5.1 Let us hear the decrees and the laws (Commandments: Before) – 64
5.7–21 You shall have no other gods but me (Commandments: Prayer) – 62
5.7–21 Lord, we will have no other God but you (Commandments: Declaration) – 63
6.6–7 The words of this book (Dedication: Presentation of a Bible) – 233
8.3 We cannot survive on bread alone (Before Reading) – 195
10.12–17 Our Lord God, we want to fear you (Acclamation) – 369
10.12–13 Fear the Lord your God, walk in his ways (Blessing) – 407
12.5–21 Lord, our God, this is the place (Approach) – 33
26.17–18 You have declared this day (Commandments: After) – 65
28.2–14 The Lord our God open his storehouse (Blessing) – 408

Joshua

1.7 Be strong and courageous (Blessing) – 409
1.7 Let us be strong and courageous (Blessing) – 410

Ruth

2.4 The Lord be with you (Greeting) – 1

1 Samuel

1.25–28 Almighty God, we bring our child (Dedication: A child) – 234
3.10 Speak, Lord, for your servant is listening* (For ourselves: Before meditation) – 256